AFTER APARTHEID

THE SOLUTION
FOR SOUTH AFRICA

AFTER APARTHEID

THE SOLUTION FOR SOUTH AFRICA

Frances Kendall and Leon Louw

ICS PRESS

ICS

Institute for Contemporary Studies
San Francisco, California

Book Design and Production by Marian Hartsough
Cover Design by Nancy Benedict
Typesetting by TBH/Typecast, Inc.

Originally published in South Africa by Amagi Publications Ltd. under the title *South Africa: The Solution*.

Inquiries, book orders, and catalog requests should be addressed to ICS Press, Institute for Contemporary Studies, 243 Kearny Street, San Francisco, CA 94108.,

Library of Congress Cataloging-in-Publication Data

Louw, Leon.
    After apartheid.

    South African ed. published under title: South Africa.
    Includes index.
    1. Social predictions—South Africa.   2. South Africa—
Social conditions.   3. South Africa—Economic conditions.
4. South Africa—Politics and government.   I. Kendall,
Frances.   II. Title.
HN801.A8L68   1987   306.0968   87-3427
ISBN 0-917616-93-6

To the Future of South Africa

TABLE OF CONTENTS

ACKNOWLEDGMENTS

THIS BOOK is the culmination of many years of research, study, thought and debate, and reflects the influence of many great thinkers, the most important of whom are Ludwig von Mises, Friedrich A. Hayek, Milton Friedman, and Murray Rothbard.

Our first thanks go to Charles Koch, who persuaded Leon to embark on this book, and helped make it possible through his financial support; also to all the other North Americans, including those at the Institute for Contemporary Studies, whose interest in and concern for South Africa have led to this American edition.

In our immediate circle of friends we are indebted to Eustace Davie, Libby Husemeyer, Terry Markman, and Michael O'Dowd for comments, insights, and ideas.

Our daughters, Justine, Camilla, and Kate, cheerfully put up with very little attention for three and a half months.

Finally, we congratulate each other for managing to preserve our marriage and our sanity under conditions of extreme stress!

PREFACE

FEW ISSUES OF U.S. FOREIGN POLICY evoke more passionate argument than the question of South Africa. About the end to be achieved—the elimination of apartheid and its replacement with a "nonracial democracy"—there is considerable consensus. But little thought is given to precisely what these terms mean. There are, after all, many forms of democracy, some better suited than others to heterogeneous societies like South Africa. Which is the best form of democracy for that country? A unitary state, on the British and French model, in which decision making is centralized and minority interests are invariably subordinated to those of the majority? Or a federal state, like West Germany's or our own, in which many decisions are made locally and minorities are protected by legal and institutional constraints on what the majority may do?

If U.S. foreign policy is to promote a negotiated settlement to the South African conflict, Americans will have to address themselves to the question of what comes *after* apartheid. It is not enough to insist that the parties sit down together and work out their differences. An impasse exists in the conflict because the two most prominent "solutions"—unqualified power for the majority (more precisely, for whomever controls the majority), and maintenance of the status quo—lead nowhere. They offer the parties no way to meet each other's demands without making unacceptable sacrifices of their most important interests. Because U.S. policy reinforces the perception that there are only two mutually exclusive alternatives, it offers no realistic hope of bringing about negotiations. Indeed, it seems likely to encourage those, both in South Africa and outside it, who believe force can or must be used to eliminate apartheid.

It has become clear to us at the Institute for Contemporary Studies that U.S. policy can do little to bring about a peaceful settlement in South Africa so long as Americans assume that there are only two possible alternatives, and so long as, in consequence, the public debate remains confined to the matter of how to compel Pretoria to hand over power to the disenfranchised majority. To find an answer to the problem of how to secure a just and democratic solution without provoking civil war, we need to ask a different question: what *form* of democracy would be best for South Africa?

Frances Kendall and Leon Louw have a solution—a decentralized political system based on the Swiss confederal model. By reformulating the problem as one of devising an arrangement in which people with diverse needs and wants can live together in harmony despite their differences, the authors open up a possibility that has escaped us, because we have assumed that a country can have only one political system, one economic system, one educational system, and so on. Their prescription for South Africa is a striking example of how institutional decentralization, combined with guarantees of equal political, civil, and economic liberty for all, can transform a seemingly insoluble "zero-sum" conflict into an opportunity for all to gain. In the arrangement Kendall and Louw propose, the game becomes "positive sum"—everyone wins.

It is this demonstration of imagination in drawing on our experience with institutions designed to respect individual freedom that recommends *After Apartheid* to anyone interested in discovering a new and more promising approach to the South African issue. Kendall and Louw's book reflects the importance of stimulating fresh thinking about persistent problems of public policy by recasting them in terms that reveal the potential of solutions based on a healthy respect for individual autonomy and free choice. In the case of South Africa, we believe such a solution is the only one that offers everyone involved in the conflict a compelling reason to cooperate in building a democratic, stable, and prosperous South Africa.

— Robert B. Hawkins, Jr.
President, Institute for Contemporary Studies

FOREWORD TO THE
SOUTH AFRICAN EDITION

AT A TIME WHEN SOUTH AFRICA is embroiled in a frantic search for an effective remedy to what the world has come to regard as one of the most vicious and morally indefensible political systems now in existence — the policy of apartheid — it is quite refreshing, hope-inspiring, and stimulating to discover two young South Africans who, as husband and wife, have come forward to offer the country a solution.

It is indeed an extremely rare occurrence to find a husband and wife who are so happily married and so intellectually intimate as to attempt to write a book together. The fact that Leon and Frances have finally succeeded in completing their manuscript is a tremendous testimony to their dedication to the search for a way towards a new South Africa of the future.

Reading through the twenty chapters of their book, *South Africa: The Solution,* was for me an absolute delight, not only because I agree with most of the positive ideas they have so clearly enunciated, but more because they have unearthed a great amount of forgotten information about blacks and whites in our country that has for many years remained hidden.

Despite the racial conflicts which have torn our country apart, it is heartening to get a positive picture about the past when the spirit of entrepreneurship, among both black and white people, existed in a climate of greater freedom and made our country the great economic power it became on the southern tip of the African continent.

What is most important and encouraging in *The Solution* is how the couple speculates and dreams about the realization of a united and prosperous South African nation of the future. They foresee that South Africa can achieve freedom for all its people in a federal system and under a constitution which contains a Bill of Rights securing the rights of all individuals.

The great problem which lies ahead of our country is surely not a lack of ideas and visions among the people of South Africa. Our most crucial challenge will remain the implementation of such bright ideas and visions. Dreamers we have galore, but it is the implementers who are few.

My fervent wish is that *The Solution* be read with interest, digested with enthusiasm, and implemented with courage.

To Leon and Frances go my sincere congratulations. And I firmly hope that they will make another effort at formulating a new strategy for determining how their solution can be put into effect in the corridors of power inside our troubled country.

—Samuel Mokgethi Motsuenyane
President, National African Federated
Chambers of Commerce (NAFCOC)

INTRODUCTION

"END APARTHEID NOW!" has become the rallying cry throughout the world of people who oppose the South African system of racial discrimination. Long unanimous in their condemnation of that system, Americans now seem increasingly ready to exert their influence to bring about its end. A recent Gallup Poll shows a majority of Americans in favor of tough economic sanctions and greater pressure on Pretoria to dismantle apartheid. Congress reflected this feeling when it overrode President Reagan's veto of legislation imposing further sanctions, as did General Motors and IBM when they announced their decisions to withdraw from South Africa.

All this activity is aimed at forcing change. But change to what? How can apartheid be dismantled without pitting race against race, without tearing apart the nation and destroying the economy? The purpose of this book is to answer these questions by offering a practical and detailed design for peaceful change to a free and just society.

Part One of the book examines some of the important historical factors that led to the present predicament. Part Two analyzes current political and economic circumstances that any workable solution must take into account. Part Three provides a comprehensive description of the political, economic, and legal systems that are necessary to achieve individual freedom, the rule of law, maximal participation in government, and protection for minorities.

We believe that South Africa will not be completely at peace until all references to ethnicity and race have been removed from the statute books. The system we propose is "colorblind," but it ensures that no one group can dominate another.

When the first edition of this book appeared in South Africa in March 1986, we hoped it would be well received and would make a valuable contribution to the debate over political reform. But we were totally unprepared for the overwhelming response it elicited. Within a few weeks the book was the number one nonfiction best-seller in the country. In the months that have followed, it has remained among the top five best-sellers. In South Africa the normal print run for a political book of this type is 2,000. A sale of 5,000 over one or two years is considered very good. Our publisher ambitiously printed 9,000 copies of *The Solution* — they sold out within six months. Since then it has been translated into Afrikaans and has set a publishing record in South Africa, far outselling any other political book of its kind. Within a year over 25,000 copies were sold.

The point is not to boast but to call attention to the real likelihood of South Africa's moving toward the solution we propose. Ordinary people everywhere are reading the book. They tell their friends, write to newspapers and magazines, and send the book to people in positions of influence. Written in jargon-free language and aimed at lay people, *The Solution* has been bought by many women in a country where economics and politics are still very much male preserves. The book is also selling well among black South Africans.

Almost daily we receive letters and phone calls from people eager to help us promote our ideas. We address groups around the country ranging from white separatists to black nationalists. Almost invariably our ideas elicit the same response — initial skepticism, followed by growing excitement and enthusiasm, and finally offers to help spread the message. One important consequence has been the establishment of an organization called *Groundswell* by Nick Taylor, a well-known and popular entertainer in South Africa. The purpose of *Groundswell* is to promote widespread awareness of and popular support for the canton proposal outlined in *The Solution*.

Groundswell is not a political organization. It is a constitutional movement that draws support from a wide variety of political groups in South Africa. Indeed, the strength of *The Solution* lies primarily in its ability to accommodate a wide variety of apparently irreconcilable political, economic, and social systems.

Naturally, there are serious stumbling blocks that will have to be overcome if our ideas are to be realized. Perhaps the most important is the fact that the current government would have to surrender most of its powers — something no government is wont to do. There is considerable evidence, however, that the South African government recognizes that the loss of much of its power is inevitable. It has already openly accepted the principles of power-sharing and devolution that are central to our proposal. The Minister of Constitutional Development and Planning, Chris Heunis, has stated that the government has made "inquiries into maximizing the devolution of powers to local authorities and minimizing central or provincial control over them." The State President has stressed that he is committed to "a democratic form of government in which all citizens will participate through their elected representatives."

The second major impediment is those politicians, both black and white, who are not interested in the well-being of South Africa but in personal aggrandizement. A decentralized system such as we propose would represent the end of their chances to seize unlimited political power.

We believe that the way to overcome these obstacles is by achieving widespread support for our ideas among the general public. To do this it will be necessary to educate people on a massive scale as to what such a system would mean, thus gaining their support and bringing about a popular movement in favor of devolution and decentralization of power. There is little question that South Africans are ready for change, and the Natal-KwaZulu Indaba is an important example of a growing tendency for people in our country to get together at a local level to solve their mutual problems.

Some people, especially those living outside South Africa, believe that, even if the system outlined in this book were to be adopted in South Africa, it would run the risk of being overthrown by a would-be dictator. We consider this very unlikely. Even now, with widespread discontent, unemployment, and rapidly rising black expectations, the military power of the present government is such that an attempted revolution would have virtually no chance of success. Given a new dispensation in South Africa brought about by widespread popular support, it is hard to envisage an attempted takeover receiving any substantial backing at all.

Although we believe there is little chance of a violent revolution occurring in South Africa, if peaceful change is not negotiated soon the future prospects for this country are gloomy indeed. If a solution to the current impasse is not found soon we can expect a continued spiral into further international isolation, increased black discontent with intensified white resistance and repression, and a weakening economy. If this happens, when negotiations finally take place in twenty or thirty years' time they will be negotiations over the future of a wasteland.

The only hope lies in a system that protects the rights and freedoms of all South Africans, regardless of race or gender, so that all can live together in peace and prosperity. The United States cannot prescribe such a solution. That is a matter for South Africans to decide. But Americans can help by encouraging the parties to the conflict to consider proposals that promise a free and just society.

South Africa has a long way to go. But energetic, creative, and intelligent people of great goodwill abound. As UDF leader Allan Boesak has observed, "change does not roll in on the wheels of inevitability. It comes through the tireless efforts and hard work of those who are willing to take the risk of fighting for freedom, democracy, and human dignity."

PART ONE

The History

*History ought to judge the past
and to instruct the contemporary
world as to the future.*
—Leopold von Ranke

Part One is a brief survey of important aspects of South
Africa's history. It aims to dispel certain prevalent myths
while revealing little-known facts that are crucial in devising a solution for South Africa's problems. These chapters highlight the sequence of events that led to the
current impasse. In doing so they focus primarily on
South Africa's two most important groups, the blacks
and the Afrikaners.

CHAPTER 1

Black South Africans:
Their Rise and Fall

*But if the men of the future are ever to break the chains of
the present they will have to understand the forces that
forged them.*

— Barrington Moore, Jr.

WHEN BLACK SOUTH AFRICANS first came into contact with the
market economy of the nineteenth century, they responded so
enthusiastically that within a few decades they were extremely
successful farmers, transport riders, artisans, and traders.

Today, few people are aware of these achievements and many
South Africans believe that blacks are naturally poor agriculturalists
who lack enterprise. It is also commonly accepted that black tribal
systems are fundamentally socialist. However, an examination of
southern African tribes reveals political and economic systems based
on individual freedom and private property rights, with considerable differences in levels of wealth and social status. Indeed, the
political systems of most of the black tribes during South Africa's
early history were similar in many respects to the canton system
which we propose for South Africa, and which, some might say, is
feasible only in a highly developed society. The freedom that characterized tribal society in part explains why blacks responded so posi-

tively to the challenges of a free market that, by the 1870s, they were outcompeting whites, especially as farmers.

But success had tragic consequences. White colonists feared black competition, and this fear, combined with the whites' desire for cheap labor, resulted in a series of laws that systematically denied blacks access to the marketplace and stripped them of any meaningful form of land ownership. This appalling sequence of events set the tone for a century of racial socialism, which led to the apparent deadlock we face today.

Tribal Society: A System of Voluntary Exchange and Private Ownership

When the first white settlers arrived in the Cape in 1652, it was occupied by the yellow-skinned Khoikhoi (Hottentots) and the San (Bushmen), and further north and east by the Cape or Southern Nguni. The Cape Nguni occupied the broad swath of territory that is present-day Ciskei, Border Region, and Transkei.

Nguni is a generic term for black-skinned people sharing a similar language structure. It includes a large number of groups and subgroups. In the Cape there are the Xhosa, the Thembu, the Mbo, and later immigrant groups such as the Mfengu. Notable among the Nguni further north are the Zulu and the Dlamini, who occupy KwaZulu and Swaziland respectively.

This chapter concentrates on the Cape Nguni because we have more detailed records of their history than of any of the other tribes. However, the political and economic systems of the other Nguni tribes and of the Sotho, Venda, and Tsonga — the peoples to the north of the Nguni with different languages and customs — although very different in detail, were similar in their fundamental structure.

Early Economy.   The Nguni people were hunters and cultivators, but they were chiefly herdsmen, and in Nguni society cattle were wealth and a medium of exchange. The men and boys who cared for the cattle were experts with a detailed knowledge of animal husbandry. Women cultivated the land, planting a variety of crops. All adult males were allotted a residential plot and land for cultivation, with a degree of security of tenure that surpasses that of the modern western freehold tradition. As long as land was not in short supply there was "commonage" (common grazing land), but this also was subject to allotment or privately held grazing rights during times when land became a scarce resource. Land allotments were made by chiefs-in-council, or headmen-in-council. There were sophisticated procedures, traditions, and laws relating to allocation, inheritance, and transfer after initial allotment.

Political and Social Structure. The Nguni lived in scattered homesteads. Among commoners these were composed of two to forty huts. A chief's homestead was usually larger, with around fifty huts or more. Each homestead was occupied by a man with his wives, his unmarried daughters, his sons and their families, and poor people who attached themselves to the headman through voluntary vassalage. By serving him, they gained access to his cattle and grazing lands. They looked to him for advice and guidance. A homestead increased in size according to its headman's reputation as a man of judgment and equity and his generosity to people poorer than himself.

In addition to the poor people who attached themselves to headmen or chiefs, there was a system of clientship whereby a poor man would be lent cattle by a wealthy community leader or chief. He herded these cattle and drank their milk, and received some of their offspring. In exchange, he assisted his benefactor in building or fencing, or attended him in a court case or in war. The influence of each Nguni chief depended on the number of his followers, and he was therefore constantly competing with his half-brothers and neighboring chiefs for new supporters.

The social structure, linked closely to the economic structure, was flexible and dynamic, with homesteads splitting from time to time, and near kinsmen building in the same neighborhood to form a loose grouping with senior kinsmen. A number of local homesteads or communities made up a village under the leadership of a headman. A group of villages in turn formed a chiefdom. The size of chiefdoms varied considerably, fluctuating and splitting to coalesce under popular leaders. A chiefdom was a political unit occupying a defined area under an independent chief. These were sometimes subdivided under subordinate leaders. For example, in 1809 the Xhosa chief Hintsa had 10,000 followers and eleven sub-chiefs.

In any local area, one clan (i.e., people all descended from a common ancestor) predominated. In any chiefdom, the chief's clan enjoyed the greatest prestige. But neither in local areas nor in chief-doms was there any exclusivity regarding clans.

Van der Kemp, the first missionary to the Nguni, reported in 1800 of the Xhosa chief Ngqika:

> He has counsellors who inform him of the sentiments of his people, and his captains admonish him with great freedom and fidelity, when he abuses his authority to such a degree, that there is reason to fear that the nation will show him their displeasure. This is done if he treats the admonition with contempt, not by way of insurrection, or taking up arms against him, but most effectually, by gradual emigration. Some kraals break up, and march towards the borders of the country. . . . They are successively followed by others, and this seldom fails to have the effect wished for. . . .[1]

Van der Kemp saw this process in action when Ngqika introduced two laws: one forbidding a man with an unfaithful wife to take the life of her seducer, and another making the chief the heir of any of his subjects who died without heirs in their direct line. Ngqika was forced to retract both these laws when his people demonstrated their disapproval by leaving. The law prohibiting revenge on a seducer was subsequently reinstated after thorough consideration. The other was not.

Followers were obliged to submit all disputes to their chief for judgment. If the chief felt that his own judgment was not competent in a given case, he would refer the parties concerned to an older and more experienced chief. People also had the right to appeal judgments in the court of a superior chief.

Hearings were usually held in open court. Proceedings were sophisticated, with ample opportunity for the arguments of all parties to be heard. Tribal courts are based on these traditions to this day.

The followers of a chief attended his council, fought for him when called upon, and paid him death duties and fines. The wealthiest men in the chiefdom had the greatest influence at the councils, where all matters were subject to lengthy discussion (or *indaba*) by all the adult men. Decisions were usually based on unanimity, so government was by consensus. On the rare occasions when unanimity was not achieved, majority rule was invoked.

In the extended family there was a traditional voluntary welfare system whereby old and sick people were cared for by the clan.

Trade.   Until the end of the eighteenth century few political and economic pressures were exerted on the Nguni by the Dutch people living in the Cape Colony. There were frequent skirmishes between the Nguni and the *trekboers* (Dutch farmers) on the eastern frontier of the Cape, and a fair amount of trading and social interaction took place, but the basic structure of the Nguni economy remained unchanged.

When the British took over the Cape Colony at the turn of the century, however, matters began to change. Where previous governments had tried to prevent interaction between colonists and Xhosas and had failed, the British sought to regulate it.

In 1817 they established a biannual trade fair at Grahamstown that Xhosas were permitted to attend. By 1824 trade fairs were being held three times a week at Fort Willshire; this meant that Xhosas were entering the Cape Colony on a regular and legal basis.

In 1829, an ordinance was passed (Ordinance 49) that formally allowed the Xhosas to cross the frontier to seek employment or attend trade fairs. To do this, however, Xhosas had to carry a pass. This system was introduced because the Cape government didn't want to prevent the influx of blacks — Cape farmers badly needed laborers — but it did want to control the influx, since more and more black refugees were moving south as a result of conquests by the powerful Zulus.

While trade at Fort Willshire continued to grow, so did the number of Xhosa poaching raids into white farms. Homesteads were burned, stock was stolen. In retaliation, white farmers led punitive expeditions into Xhosa territory.

Successive British governments tried many different policies in an attempt to end the warfare on the Eastern Front. One of these proposed the establishment of a buffer zone — an unoccupied strip

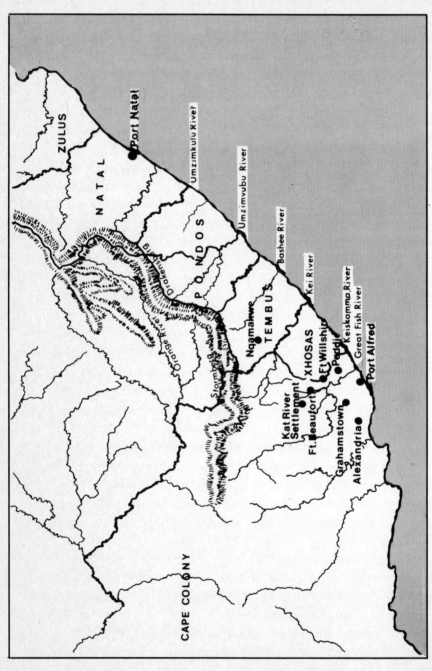

Map 1 Eastern Cape—1880s

of neutral territory—between the colonists and the Xhosa. Another recommended the creation of a dense band of settlement along the frontier to discourage Xhosa raids. One of the settlements created for this purpose was that of the Mfengu.

The Mfengu Entrepreneurs. In 1835, 16,000 Mfengu with 22,000 head of cattle formally entered the Cape Colony at Governor D'Urban's bidding and were settled in the Peddie District. The Mfengu were Natal blacks who had been displaced by the rise of the Zulu Kingdom, and D'Urban was perfectly candid about his reasons for importing them:

> The Fingo community would supply military support against Mintza, the Xhosa paramount chief; the colony would gain the labor of sober, industrious people, well skilled in the tasks of herding and agriculture; the land in the Peddie district to which they were moved was worse than useless, but, he confidently expected, would be turned into a flourishing garden by the newcomers.[2]

The Mfengu responded spectacularly to the opportunites and incentives of the market economy. On arrival in Peddie, they entered agricultural service as cattle herders and shepherds, and were engaged in tilling, ploughing, and reaping. But they very soon put their newfound skills to use on their own behalf. They used their wages to invest in sheep, wagons, and tools, and were rewarded with land for fighting in the Cape Army.

They also formed a close association with Methodist missionaries who keenly favored the spread of black agriculture and who provided training and encouragement. The doyen of South African missionaries, the Reverend John Philip, argued that if the blacks were allowed to accumulate and develop land they would be peacefully integrated into the colonial economy. He called for a laissez-faire policy toward the Khoikhoi, Xhosa, and Mfengu, insisting that it would make them more productive farmers. He also maintained that the abolition of slavery would improve, not worsen, the labor market.

So the Mfengu could be found not only farming their own land, but also working on small holdings on mission stations. Before long they were engaged in trade and transport too. By the 1840s and 1850s they were selling tobacco, firewood, cattle, and milk, and disposing of surplus grain for cash or stock.

At this time the Mfengu, the Hottentots, and Coloureds who had settled at Kat River were making the most rapid advances in peasant agriculture. However, other successful farming activities, also encouraged by the missionaries, were under way elsewhere in the Eastern Cape. By the end of the century, the Thembu in the Transkei rivaled the Mfengu as farmers and landowners.

In 1858, Governor George Grey issued a proclamation permitting blacks to buy grain land at £1 ($12) per acre.[3] By 1864, 508 blacks had bought 16,200 acres, while a further 106 rented 6,000 acres from the government. A large number of blacks (squatters) also leased land from white farmers in exchange for labor, cash, or produce. By the 1870s, black farmers in the Eastern Cape were active and prosperous. The Mfengu competed against white farmers at agricultural shows and won many prizes. A Wesleyan missionary told the 1865 Commission on Native Affairs: "Even this year [after the drought] I think their exhibition far surpassed that of the Europeans. It was a universal remark in the district that the Fingo exhibition far excelled that of the Europeans both as to number and quality of the articles exhibited."[4] A Cape statistician noted: "Taking everything into consideration, the native district of Peddie surpasses the European district of Albany in its productive powers."[5] In the Transkei, a black community raised £4,500 ($50,000)* in three years to build a school in Blythswood, and contributed £2,000 ($20,000) toward bridges and roads through the territory. Headmen attended the opening of the bridge over the Kei to demonstrate their appreciation of improved transport facilities.

In the 1870s a flourishing group of black transport riders developed. Many farmers turned to transport riding once their crops had been harvested. There were also "master tradesmen . . . in constant work [with] apprentices," artisans, contractors, and builders. Commentators of the time described the blacks as "very industrious," "very thrifty," "greatly progressing," with "a desire to have their children educated." It was observed that "freedom from restraint is a ruling passion in them."[6]

---

* The dollar figures in parenthesis are rough estimates of the value in current U.S. dollars.

During this period, the purchasing power of blacks in the Eastern Cape exceeded £400,000 ($4.5 million) a year. Exports were many and varied, including angora hair, hides, horns, goat and sheep skins, tobacco, grain, and cattle valued at £750,000 ($9 million) per annum.

A missionary in the Thembu area described the local shops:

> Now things are very different and every shop has some kind of European clothing. . . . Yes, and not ordinary apparel such as coats, trousers, boots, stuff for making ordinary dresses, but often you will find a shop as well supplied in the heart of Kaffirland as in many a shop in the Colony . . . soap, candles, tea, coffee, cocoa and sugar, blue starch, ladies' kid boots, ready-made mantles, shawls, bonnets and hats (ready trimmed). All these sorts of things are to be purchased in the kaffir traders' shops. Also scents, scented soaps, jewelry, etc.[7]

Black farmers were becoming extremely diversified in their produce: ". . . At an agricultural show held in Nqamakwe, Fingoland, in 1880, prizes were awarded for wheat, barley, oats, potatoes, sweet potatoes, forage, maize, sorghum, tobacco, cabbages, turnips, beets, wool, bread, butter, dried fruit, cheese, bacon, ham and handicrafts."[8] By 1890 there were many progressive black commercial farmers who had purchased their farms outright. They invested much of their profits in fences, walls, irrigation, and improved stock breeds, and adopted the most advanced farming methods of the time. They lived in brick houses (built by Europeans) and stocked them with furniture, crockery, cutlery, stationery, and so on. They sent their children to multiracial boarding schools and employed laborers and leased portions of their land. They were the mainstay of agricultural societies and associations, owning farms of up to 1,710 morgen (about 3,600 acres).

By 1890 there were between one thousand and two thousand of these affluent black commercial farmers. Now, one hundred years later, you will have difficulty finding even one.

What Went Wrong?

In the district of Herschel in the northeastern corner of the Cape, as elsewhere, a healthy black farming community developed in the nineteenth century. In 1873, over and above their own requirements, black farmers produced 1,000 bales of wool, 6,000 bags of wheat, and 30,000 bags of "kaffir corn" and mealies.

Yet in the 1940s a Franciscan priest touring the district described Herschel as follows: "A lot of the area is mountainous and most of the rest is badly eroded, so there is not much left for cultivation. . . . There is virtually no work in the whole area. . . . All forms of malnutrition are obviously a problem throughout the Reserve."[9] In the Keiskama river valley today, productivity is lower than it was in the 1870s, despite a R20 million government-funded irrigation scheme and heavy subsidies.

Where once black farmers took with alacrity to the market economy, western technology, literacy, and the use of money, and competed as equals with immigrant farmers from Germany and England, there is now poverty, malnutrition, and stagnation. Where whites were once dazzled by black entrepreneurship, they now look disparagingly at blacks, and pronounce them inherently bad farmers and poor entrepreneurs.

What went wrong? Why did blacks do so well in the Eastern Cape, and indeed throughout South Africa, in the nineteenth century and fail so badly in the twentieth?

Have blacks retrogressed over the past 100 years? Have agricultural and climatic conditions deteriorated? No—the answer lies in changes in their economic and political conditions. Until the last two decades of the nineteenth century, blacks enjoyed a considerable degree of economic freedom; in this century they have been allowed almost none. How did this come about?

The truth is that white farmers felt threatened by blacks. Not only were blacks better farmers but they were also competing with white farmers for land. Moreover, they were self-sufficient and hence not available to work on white farms or in industry, particularly in the Transvaal gold mines where their labor was badly needed. As a result, a series of laws was passed that robbed blacks of almost all economic freedom. The purpose of these laws was to prevent blacks from competing with whites and to drive them into the work force. This was the beginning of the "black socialism" that exists throughout South Africa today.

A People Dispossessed

During the nineteenth century white expansion and black migration increased the demand for land and the eastern boundary of the Cape Colony moved further and further eastward. The areas allotted to blacks became smaller and smaller.

We have seen that by the 1870s blacks had purchased or been granted crown land as well as land in mission reserves. Many of them also leased land from white farmers in exchange for cash or labor. During this period, white landowners were experiencing a severe shortage of labor. The blacks and Hottentots preferred self-employment or working for higher wages in the towns to being agricultural laborers.

To "remedy the evil" the Cape Assembly passed a series of Location Acts in 1869, 1876, and 1884 to reduce the number of "squatters" in white-owned lands. These "idle squatters" were the black farmers we have mentioned, who rented land from white farmers and developed it for themselves. The purpose of the legislation was to prevent them from being self-sufficient so that they would be forced to become wage laborers.

However, many white farmers were perfectly happy to lease land to blacks in exchange for labor, so the anti-squatter legislation was largely evaded and the shortage of labor continued. In 1893 the Cape Labour Commission was appointed to look into the matter. When the commissioners asked why there was a labor shortage they were told: "The natives are independent. They have land and grow what they choose, and their wants are extremely small." In Alice a white farmer said that the blacks "seem to be able to raise sheep here, the Europeans not." In Alexandria and Stutterheim "the native can live by agriculture, but not the white man." In Port Alfred they were told: "Europeans cannot compete with natives. The labour kills them."[10]

The rise of the gold and diamond mining, transport, construction, and service industries throughout South Africa increased the need and competition for cheap labor. Mine owners knew there would be no cheap labor as long as blacks had access to land. In 1911 the President of the Chamber of Mines in Johannesburg explained: "[The black] cares nothing if industries pine for want of labor when his crops and home-brewed drink are plentiful." He called for a policy to compel blacks to enter the labor force and urged the government to do "everything to encourage the native to be a wage earner by extending the policy of splitting into family holdings land now held in the native reserves under tribal tenure."[11]

Thus both white farmers and mine owners realized that the black man's independence had to be broken if he was to supply their labor requirements. The colonial government was ready and willing to help them and a series of laws was introduced to achieve their ends thoroughly and systematically.

Act 33 of 1892 put the onus on the white farmer to register blacks on his farm. The number of blacks living on his farm and not earning a wage (tenants) was restricted. If that number was exceeded he had to pay a fine. As a direct consequence of this act a number of black "squatters" were turned off the land and suffered great losses of stock, homes, cultivated fields, and other possessions. However, as in the case of the Location Acts, Act 33 was widely evaded.

In 1894, the Glen Grey Act drawn up by Cape Premier Cecil Rhodes became law. The Act was popular among socialists because it provided for individual land tenure in black reserves on the basis of equal distribution. It did this by splitting the reserves into agricultural holdings of ten acres each. No man was allowed to own more than one lot. The act was intended to make the reserves self-supporting and to boost the labor supply. The government was well aware that ten acres of poor land could not provide for the needs of one family, and that most of the men would be forced out of the reserves onto the labor market.

In addition, the ten-acre limitation prevented black farmers from competing with whites, because it made it impossible for any black farmer to expand his holdings. Black commercial farmers were well aware of this, and strongly protested the violation of their property rights. Charles Pamla, one of the most influential black spokesmen, observed: "No man is allowed to occupy more than one lot. This shuts out all improvements and industry of some individuals who may work and buy. . . . Surely Mr. Rhodes can't expect that all natives will be equal. He himself is richer than others; even trees differ in height."[12]

Further anti-squatting legislation was introduced. Act 30 of 1899 permitted whites to employ any number of blacks and made them buy licenses costing £36 ($400) per annum before they could lease land to blacks. The cost of the licenses was passed on to blacks in the form of prohibitively high rents. Despite all these laws, many white farmers continued to rent land to blacks illegally, so Act 32 of 1909 was passed. This raised license fees and tightened the definition of bona fide laborers.

Eventually these laws achieved their ends. Sharecroppers (blacks farming white land and sharing the produce) and lessees were evicted. Black farmers became wage laborers. Many of those forced off white land moved to the black reserves, where competition for the ten-acre plots increased dramatically. When John X. Merriman, head of the South African Party in the Cape, was asked if he would drive blacks onto white farms as laborers, he replied: "I would not drive them, but they will drive themselves when they get congested in land held under individual tenure."[13]

Finally came the notorious Native Land Act of 1913, which designated 8 percent of South Africa's surface area as "Native Reserves." Blacks were forbidden to buy land in white areas (the remaining 92 percent) and whites were prohibited from buying land in the reserves (where blacks had the limited title described above). In addition, sharecropping and the renting of white farm land by blacks were forbidden. Only bona fide black farm laborers could live on white farms. (The Native Land Act is discussed in more detail in the next chapter.)

White farmers who had previously evaded anti-squatter legislation were eventually seduced into accepting the laws aimed at driving blacks into the reserves and into wage labor by a massive program of subsidies, grants, and other aid. This took the form of assistance for fencing, dams, and houses, as well as generous rail rates, special credit facilities, and bountiful tax relief. In 1908 an economist, F. B. Smith, remarked: "It is probable that during the last twenty years more money per head of the rural population has been devoted to the relief of farmers in South Africa than any country in the world."[14]

A number of other factors penalized black farmers. Railways and good roads did not run into the black areas, so it was difficult and expensive to transport goods to markets. They had to sell their produce to licensed white traders in the reserves. Because these traders were granted a monopoly for an area with a radius of five miles, they were able to charge more than 20 percent above market prices while buying from the black farmers at well below market price.

After an epidemic of East Coast fever (a cattle disease), black farmers were allowed to sell their cattle only to white traders with government concessions. Again, the traders' response to their monopoly was to make offers at well below market prices for the stock. Inevitably, this encouraged overstocking. Overcrowding on the small plots prevented rotational grazing and hastened soil erosion.

People soon forgot the impressive achievements of blacks prior to the turn of the century, and it became conventional wisdom that "blacks are bad farmers," "blacks lack motivation," and "blacks are not entrepreneurs." Throughout South Africa, the history of blacks followed a pattern depressingly similar to that of the Cape.

Natal

The *Natal Witness* of April 1, 1870 had reported: "Perhaps the most striking feature in the Kaffir character is his energy and industry as a farmer. The thousands of acres that have been ploughed up by Kaffirs, and the hundreds of wagons they possess, are conclusive proof of their readiness and fitness to become agriculturists."[15] In 1880 regulations were passed allowing the sale of land to blacks, and in the following decade blacks bought 67,077 acres for £36,412 ($430,000). Between January 1890 and July 1891 they bought a further 56,000 acres for £34,000 ($400,000).

But between 1890 and 1910, with the rising demand on the gold fields for agricultural products, railway lines were built to serve white farming areas. Also, white farmers were subsidized in many ways through the Agricultural Development Acts of 1904 and 1907. With the help of these subsidies, the value of white farm land rose and it became less rewarding to lease land to blacks, who received no subsidies. White landowners no longer needed black tenants, so rents were pushed up. Marginal black tenants left the land spontaneously. Those blacks who had no binding contracts or title deeds were simply evicted. Even where this did not happen, blacks were afraid to make improvements because of the uncertainty of their tenure.

A number of levies and fees were imposed on blacks, with the result that they paid a higher percentage of their income in taxes than whites. The 1913 Land Act brought all these pressures to a logical conclusion. Commercial tenants were reduced to wage laborers. Mr. Nkantolo, giving evidence to the Natal Native Affairs Commission in 1906, summed up the situation:

> The money they paid was thrown into a big tank that never seemed to fill. What surprised them was that whilst on the one hand they were heavily taxed by government, on the other hand, they were called upon to pay high rentals by private land-owners. The Government had them by the head, and the farmers by the legs. . . . The Natives had no means of making wealth.[16]

Transvaal and Orange Free State (OFS)

By 1904, 750,000 blacks in the Transvaal were renting private land and crown land or farming their own. Some 123,000 were in the reserves and only 50,000 were unemployed. This number of unemployed is so low that we may say the Transvaal had full employment, with 77 percent of the black population owning or renting land.

By the 1890s there was a widely established practice of "farming-on-the-halves" in the Free State. This was a form of sharecropping in which whites provided seed and land, blacks farmed the grain, and the returns were shared. This caused many complaints among white landowners who didn't practice sharecropping and disliked the competition from blacks, who, as we have seen, tended to be more effective farmers.

The 1904 Labour Commission commented that black farmers were competing with whites and causing labor to be withheld from industry. In both states, a series of anti-squatting measures was passed, and finally the 1913 Land Act reduced the rent-payers and sharecroppers to low-wage laborers, and did away with the system of "farming-on-the-halves."

A Golden Age Forgotten

Thus ended a brief golden era for black South Africans. For a few short decades they were allowed to experience a relatively free market, unfettered land ownership, modern technology, equality at law, reasonable freedom of movement, and unrestricted upward mobility for the enterprising. They responded magnificently.

One of the reasons they progressed with such alacrity is unquestionably the congruity between their traditional ways and the market economy—a fact that has eluded virtually every contemporary analyst. Pre-colonial African law and custom shared the following features with the free market system:

- Assets such as stock, crops, huts, handicrafts, and weapons were privately owned and land was privately allotted or subject to private grazing rights;

- There were no laws against free contract and voluntary exchange;

- There was no coercive redistribution of wealth and almost no taxes;

- Chiefs and headmen had few autocratic powers and usually needed to obtain full consensus for decisions;

- Central government was limited, with a high degree of devolution to village councils, and there was no central planning structure;

- There were no powers of arbitrary expropriation, and land and huts could be expropriated only under extreme conditions after a full public hearing.

Today it is said that black tradition and temperament call for "African socialism." Many current political leaders maintain that blacks can be properly fed and housed only through massive state redistribution and welfare. In our view, such measures would be in direct conflict with black tradition and would lead to greater poverty and more misery than blacks currently endure.

The only way to break the chains that shackle South Africa's blacks is to repeal forthwith all the laws that discriminate against blacks. If they are free to participate fully in a market economy, within a few years there will be an explosion of economic growth in South Africa that will astonish the world.

CHAPTER 2

The Rise of Afrikanerdom

Seek in the past all that is fine and noble and build your future on it.

— President Paul Kruger

THE HISTORY OF THE AFRIKANERS is the history of a people's struggle to free themselves from government interference so that they might live according to their own values. But this heritage of individualism and the pursuit of freedom has been largely forgotten.

In the course of the twentieth century, the Afrikaner nation has become inextricably linked with the concept of the paternalistic state and powerful central government. Now the Afrikaners have taken on the role of interventionist and it is the blacks who are fighting for their rights. Ironically, these rights represent much the same freedoms for which the Afrikaners formerly shed their blood.

The time has come for Afrikaners to rediscover the true principles of democracy and limited government that were held so dear by the *Voortrekker* and his forebears, because these are the only principles on which a system can be built that will offer freedom to all South Africans regardless of race.

The Origin of the Afrikaner Nation

Since 1948, the Afrikaners have dominated the political scene in South Africa with formidable purpose. They have earned the world's condemnation, but also its grudging respect. Whatever their faults, weakness has not been among them.

Their beginnings were remarkably inauspicious: their earliest forebears were no more than a handful of freed servants. Nonetheless, the desire for self-rule that created the powerful nation of today was present from the start and has formed a dominant and recurring theme throughout South Africa's history.

On the 7th of April 1652, an expedition of about ninety men, led by Jan van Riebeeck, went ashore at Table Bay near the southern tip of Africa. They had been sent by the Dutch East India Company (Vereenighde Oostindische g'octrooijeerde Compagnie—V.O.C.) of the Batavian Republic to "provide that the . . . East India ships, to and from Batavia . . . may [procure] . . . herbs, flesh, water, and other needful refreshments—and by this means restore the health of their sick."[1]

Van Riebeeck was instructed to establish a garrison (the Fort of Good Hope), plant fruit trees, create a vegetable garden, and breed livestock. This was no easy task. The men who had been sent to the Cape with him were expected to work hard under rigid discipline and often on short rations. Many deserted and others worked unwillingly and carelessly.

Van Riebeeck decided that the solution to the problem was to turn over certain activities to private enterprise. As a consequence, some of the Company servants were freed and given land to grow vegetables and later to undertake tavern-keeping, milling, woodcutting, hunting, fishing, tailoring, and even medical practices, usually under licensed monopolies granted by the V.O.C. Van Riebeeck also suggested to the Company that families be imported from Batavia to grow corn and rear livestock.

The first nine freed servants (free burghers) were settled in the Liesbeeck Valley on Khoikhoi grazing land in 1657. The Khoikhoi (commonly known as Hottentots) were indigenous yellow-skinned nomadic herders who grazed their cattle on the lush pasture of the Cape each spring. They objected strongly to the arrival of the farmers on their grazing land, and the first of many skirmishes over land between whites and people of color broke out.

During peace negotiations in 1660, Van Riebeeck informed the Khoikhoi that they had lost part of their grazing land as a consequence of war, and he had a hedge of bitter almond trees planted across the Cape Flats to cut off 6,000 acres of the Cape Peninsula from the interior. The Khoikhoi and the whites were kept separate by this hedge and both were forbidden to cross it. This was the first apartheid measure in South Africa.

The Seeds of Afrikanerdom

The number of settler farmers grew rapidly, but the Company never had any intention of granting them real freedom. Their activities were rigidly controlled. They were forbidden to trade with anyone other than the Company. Laws against trading with the Khoikhoi were especially strict. The Company bought their produce at fixed prices and told them what they could and could not farm. In 1658 they staged their first "strike," declaring: "It is too hard that they are compelled to plant . . . this or that, . . . to refrain from following their own bent, and from bartering all sorts of things from the natives . . . to sell . . . to the ships. . . . We will not be slaves to the Company."[2]

These men who were demanding freedom were the forebears of the Afrikaners. They were mainly Dutch and Low German, in a ratio of about two to one, with a sprinkling of Scandinavians and Frenchmen. Most of them were adventurers who had been lured into service with the V.O.C. by vague promises of eventual riches. Many had been displaced by wars in Europe and had experienced a long history of repression.

After 1688 they were joined by about 200 French Huguenot refugees who came to the Cape assisted by the Company. To facilitate their rapid assimilation, the French were interspersed among the Dutch and German farmers and Dutch was the only language used in public schools. By the end of the seventeenth century there was a clear distinction between Afrikaners — burghers who regarded the Cape as their permanent home, and Europeans — Company servants who were temporary residents.

The Trekboers

Company government in the Cape was inefficient and corrupt. The Council of Policy (the legislative body) levied taxes on the burghers and fixed low prices for their produce, which they could still sell only to the Company. The burghers had no representation in government.

Despite a V.O.C. ruling preventing Company officials from farming and trading privately, they did so with impunity. All distribution was undertaken by monopolies granted and controlled by the Governors, who used their powers to protect their own interests. Not surprisingly, they became extremely rich. In addition, the market for produce was virtually confined to Cape Town and visiting ships. By the early eighteenth century, with both the burghers and the Company officials farming, there was a hopeless oversupply. As a consequence, more and more burghers turned to stock farming, and the stock-owners migrated further and further inland, away from Cape officialdom and taxes. These farmers came to be known as Trekboers.

The government tried frantically to stop the Trekboers. Periodically it proclaimed boundaries beyond which settlement was illegal, on pain of confiscation of cattle and twelve months' hard labor. But the Trekboers ignored it. These pioneering farmers were rugged and independent spirits who moved on if they were annoyed by wild animals, hostile tribes, or tax collectors. They were isolated and self-reliant and became increasingly resentful and contemptuous of the feeble attempts made by Company officials to impose regulations on them.

The Cape Patriots

By the end of the eighteenth century there were almost 20,000 white colonists in the Cape, and highly placed officials in the Cape were once again threatening the livelihood of the free burghers.

During this period the burghers were influenced by the writings of prominent European philosophers who espoused democratic ideals, such as Locke, Montesquieu, and Rousseau. In particular they were influenced by John Locke, who believed that all persons have the right to own property, to think and express themselves freely, and to worship as they please. Political authority over the individual is limited, and is justified only by the need to serve the common good. According to Locke, government is a trust that is forfeited when it exceeds those bounds and becomes oppressive.

These ideas, together with the success of the American Revolution, encouraged the burghers to make their first demands for the political rights that would protect their economic interests. They called themselves the Patriots and attended secret meetings and distributed pamphlets suggesting that people are entitled to replace an oppressive regime with a new one.

In 1779 they petitioned the Directors of the Company, demanding representation in government and on the Council of Justice, the right to export and import freely and to sell on the open market, and the right to trade with the Company without intervention. The Cape Patriots failed to attain their main aims, but the movement instilled in Afrikaners the important and basic democratic ideas that people have the right to elect and dismiss their governments and that inviolable laws should protect people from official whims.

In the border districts of Swellendam and Graaff-Reinet the burghers had far more freedom to vent their dissatisfaction with the Company. In 1795 the Graaff-Reinet burghers ordered the *landdrost* (the Company official) to leave, and refused to obey Company laws or pay Company taxes. Swellendam followed Graaff-Reinet's example and the two districts declared their intention of governing themselves: "We have been long enough under the Yoke of Slavery and are now resolved to venture the last drop of blood of our dear Fatherland and resort under a Free Republic."[3]

British Rule and Policies Leading to the Great Trek

The years between 1795 and 1806 were a period of political transition in which the Cape was governed first by the British, then by the Batavian Republic, and again by the British, who occupied the Cape for the second time in 1806.

British colonial policy was influenced heavily by the French Revolution and the American War of Independence. The government was in no degree prepared to understand or sympathize with the aspirations of "the people." As a result, British policies over the thirty years from 1834 onwards led inexorably to a mass exodus of Afrikaners from the Cape. This emigration, called the Great Trek, was a profoundly significant milestone in South Africa's history.

One hundred fifty years of weak Company rule had left the Cape Dutch and, more particularly, the Trekboers in the interior largely to their own devices. The Trekboers had opened up the interior, protected themselves from cattle raids and attacks by indigenous peoples, made roads, and educated their children on their own. They had also developed their own language—Afrikaans. They were obstinate and individualistic and their only requirement of any government was that it should leave them alone.

The colonial government, however, had no intention of doing this. On the contrary, its primary aim was to import English immigrants and anglicize the Cape. It set out to achieve this by various measures.

Under Company rule the burghers had experienced a certain degree of self-government. The collegial institutions serving this purpose were not abolished. In 1813, Governor Cradock announced that all future official appointments would depend on a knowledge of English. From 1814 onwards, and especially after the arrival of English settlers in 1820, English-speaking officials were appointed in increasing numbers and favored in many ways. In 1822, English became the sole official language of the Cape.

The Afrikaners' Dutch Reformed Church was brought under British rule and the English Governor made head of the church. Cradock ordered prayers to be read at every service for the British royal family and for British victory at war. Vacancies in the Dutch Reformed Church were filled with English-speaking ministers, and the church was opened to Hottentots and blacks, a measure that conflicted directly with the religious beliefs of the burghers. (It was the sincere conviction of the Afrikaners that the Bible forbade them to consort with heathens, that the children of Ham (i.e., people of color) were condemned to perpetual servitude, and that it was part of their covenant with God that whites should be the guardians of blacks.)

Philanthropists in England put powerful pressure on the colonial office to stop practices that resulted in other races being subordinated to whites. One of the results of their pressure was the establishment of the Circuit Court of 1812, later known as the Black Circuit. The purpose of the Black Circuit was to investigate allegations of cruel treatment and over a hundred alleged murders of Hottentots by colonists. Not a single murder charge was upheld and the trials proved that there was very little justification for the allegations, but the Black Circuit caused a furor among the Cape Dutch. They considered it a gross affront that they should have been falsely accused by servants, and felt that even though most of the accused had been acquitted, their good name had been besmirched.

The activities of the Black Circuit culminated in the Slagtersnek tragedy. When a frontier burgher named Frederik Bezuidenhout ignored repeated summonses to appear in court in connection with the alleged ill-treatment of his Hottentot servant, Hottentot soldiers were sent to arrest him. When he resisted, he was shot dead. His brother Johannes swore to avenge him and led a rebellion of about sixty men that was speedily crushed. Five of the ringleaders were hanged. (Four of them had to ascend the scaffold a second time because the rope broke.) To some frontier Boers, Slagtersnek became a symbol of the oppression Afrikaners suffered.

In 1833, slaves in the Cape were emancipated. Compensation was offered on the same basis as for West Indian slaves, although Cape slaves were twice as valuable on the market as West Indian slaves. In addition, compensation in the form of government bonds had to be collected in person at the Bank of England in London. A commission of 12 percent had to be paid by those who wanted to receive their compensation in Cape Town. As a result, English speculators traveled into the interior buying up compensation claims at huge discounts. Many burghers were crippled by the financial losses they incurred. "Nearly all the Trekkers who have left records mentioned this, as a rule carefully explaining that it was not emancipation as such but the way in which it was carried out that hurt them."[4]

The Afrikaner farmers on the eastern frontier had suffered severe losses as a result of a series of wars with the Xhosas from the late eighteenth century onwards. The Boers (farmers) received no help from the government and relied on the protective or punitive power of burgher commandos to protect themselves from ruinous

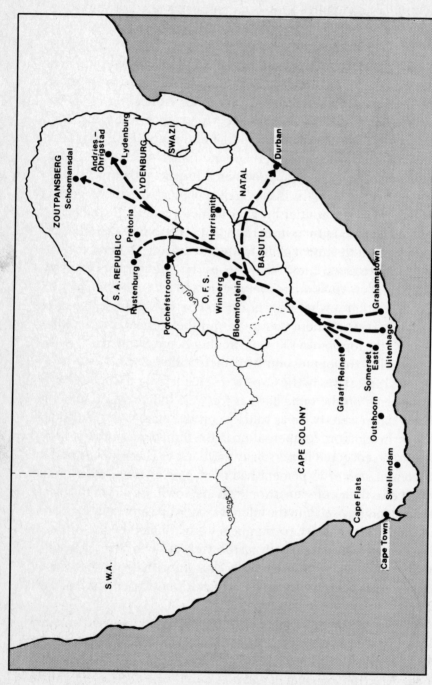

Map 2 Great Trek

raids. Now the commando system was banned and the farmer was bereft of any means of self-defense.

It was a combination of these factors — the colonial anglicization policy, the lack of representation in government, enforced equality between burghers and their servants in their homes and churches, lack of compensation for their slaves, and lack of support in the border wars — that finally brought about the massive revolt of Afrikanerdom against British rule: the Great Trek.

The Great Trek, 1834-1854

The Great Trek was an organized exodus of many thousands of Afrikaner frontier farmers from the British Cape Colony to the neighboring territories to the north and northeast. It was not a spontaneous folk-migration. It was the best solution a group of Afrikaner frontier leaders could devise to enable a portion of frontier society to withdraw from what they considered an intolerable situation.

Most of the Voortrekkers came from the frontier districts because the Trekboers who lived there were accustomed to loading up their possessions and moving to new pastures. As we have seen, they had become excellent and resilient pioneers but very impatient members of an organized state. The Great Trek was not, however, simply an acceleration of the Trekboer movement. Some of the Trekboers remained loyalists, albeit tenuously so, whereas the Voortrekker was a rebel looking for a permanent home in an independent republic. The leaders of the Great Trek were Louis Trichardt and Hans van Rensburg, who opened the way to the Transvaal Lowveld and Portuguese East Africa; Andries Hendrik Potgieter, who founded a settlement in the far north; and Gert Maritz and Piet Retief.

These leaders impressed upon the other Boers that, once they crossed the Cape frontier, they would be free of British control and could pursue their own material and spiritual values in their own republics. They would be able to fulfill the ideals of self-government and personal freedom that had been advocated by the old Cape Patriots and that were being implemented in North America. "The idea of an Afrikaner state acted as a clarion-call to the frontiersman, and aroused the imagination of the idealist. It transformed the Trek from a reckless rebellion into a divinely inspired mission in Africa."[5]

In 1837, an historic document appeared in the *Grahamstown Journal* explaining the main causes of the great emigration. This was Retief's Manifesto, and it is regarded as the authentic voice of the Great Trek:

> We are resolved, wherever we go, that we will uphold the just principles of liberty. . . . No-one shall be held in a state of slavery [but we will] preserve proper relations between master and servant . . . We will not molest any people, nor deprive them of the smallest property, but if attacked, we shall consider ourselves fully justified in defending our persons and effects. . . . We make known that when we shall have framed a code of laws for our future guidance, copies shall be forwarded to the colony for general information. . . . We propose in the course of our journey, and on arriving at the country in which we shall permanently reside, to make known to the native tribes our intentions, and our desire to live in peace and friendly intercourse with them. . . . We are now quitting the fruitful land of our birth, in which we have suffered enormous losses and continued vexation, and are entering a wild and dangerous territory; but we go with firm reliance on an all-seeing, just, and merciful Being, Whom it will be our endeavor to fear and humbly to obey.[6]

Voortrekker Republics

More than a dozen Voortrekker republics were established outside of the Cape Colony, and all were characterized by a high degree of individual autonomy and severely limited central government. One of the first was De Vrye Province van Nieuw Holland in Zuid Oost Afrika, popularly known as Natalia. A constitution was drawn up in 1838 and a Volksraad of twenty-four members elected. The Volksraad had little stability, however, and basically every person acted as he wished. Natalia's independence was shortlived. The republic was annexed by the British in 1843 and many of the Voortrekkers left again on a second trek.

The most extreme example of this independence was Klein Vrystaat (1886–1891), a miniature republic established in the Eastern Transvaal. It was a constitutional anarchy having no formal government. There could not be a more unambiguous statement of Boer anti-government sentiment.

The Transvaal

Several republics were established in what was to become the Transvaal. Some were never formally proclaimed, others had no written
constitution. Often they were nothing more than spontaneous settlements with ad hoc administration. The Boers prided themselves
on having acquired their land by agreement with local chiefs. (As
the chiefs did not always comprehend fully what was involved, there
were often serious misunderstandings.) These trekker communities
were fiercely independent and none of them was willing to be ruled
by another. In 1849, however, Andries Pretorius persuaded them to
form the *Verenigde Bond:* a "United Bond of the entire community
on this side of the Vaal River."

In 1852, at the Sand River Convention, the British recognized
the right of Afrikaners north of the Vaal River to "manage their own
affairs and govern themselves according to their own laws." The Zuid
Afrikaansche Republiek—popularly known as the Transvaal—was
formed.

In 1857 a constitution based in part on the constitution of the
United States was drawn up by the Transvaalers. It provided for an
elected Volksraad with legislative power. The republic was divided
into six field-cornetcies, each consisting of 60 to 100 households.
There was a land tax on farms and a tax on ammunition sales. Only
the Dutch Reformed Church was officially recognized. Foreigners
and people of color were not accepted as citizens, and Englishmen,
Germans, and especially missionaries were discouraged from settling in the territory.

The freedoms the Afrikaners believed in and were prepared to
fight for were the freedom of the family to do what it wanted on
its own property, the freedom of the group to regulate common
affairs, and the freedom of the entire community to control its own
affairs. Thus freed, the people of the Transvaal remained happy for
many years. The Volksraad met here and there but had no money
to do anything. The people were guided by their own dictates and
by what was socially acceptable.

In 1877, the Transvaal was annexed by the British, who charged
that there was chaos, that the government was not functioning
properly, and that annexation was for the good of the Boers. In truth,

the Boers simply had a healthy disrespect for regulations and taxes, and were content with their "sketchy administrative system."[7]

The Transvaal fought for independence under the triumvirate of Paul Kruger, Piet Joubert, and M.W. Pretorius, and in 1881 the republic was restored under Paul Kruger.

Orange Free State

The area between the Orange and Vaal rivers was occupied by the Boers in much the same way as the Transvaal. In 1848 it was annexed by the British and called the Orange River Sovereignty, but six years later was granted freedom at the Bloemfontein Convention under the name of the Orange Free State.

A provisional government and twenty-nine representatives drafted a constitution based on the French constitution of 1848, with clauses from the American constitution. The legislative body was a Volksraad elected to a four-year term. The Volksraad was not allowed to pass laws that interfered with the right of the inhabitants to assemble peacefully. Private property rights and freedom of the press were guaranteed. Citizens had the right to petition the government to introduce, revise, or revoke a law. Essentially, there was only one statute, the *Wetboek*, which could be amended. Like the Transvaal, the Free State did not grant citizenship to white *uitlanders* (foreigners) or to people of color. Justice was administered according to the liberal principles of Roman-Dutch Common Law. Sir John Henry Brand became President of the Free State in 1864, and during his twenty-five year presidency it came to be regarded as a model republic.

Conclusion

The traditions of blacks and Afrikaners living in Southern Africa in the nineteenth century differed in many ways, but they shared certain important elements. In both, if people didn't like the rules governing their local community, they could freely move off and join another. Both were characterized by minimum central government and numerous small autonomous communities in which people were intimately involved in decisions regarding their own lives.

CHAPTER 3

The Rise of Apartheid

The past thirty years have seen the greatest number of laws restricting our rights and progress, until today we have reached a stage where we have almost no rights at all.
— Chief Albert Luthuli, 1952

IN SOUTH AFRICA AND ABROAD the concept of apartheid is firmly linked with Afrikaner nationalism. Most people believe that the Afrikaners both invented and implemented apartheid, and are entirely to blame for it. This is untrue.

The first apartheid law was passed in 1660, only a few years after whites arrived in the Cape, when Van Riebeeck planted his hedge of bitter almonds to keep the Hottentots and free burghers apart. The first separate school for blacks was established in 1663, and in 1678 the V.O.C. forbade all inter-racial "concubinage" on pain of up to three years' imprisonment with hard labor on Robben Island. In 1681 the V.O.C. issued prohibitions forbidding whites to attend parties with slave (black) women, and when there was an inland expedition, it issued a special regulation forbidding sex between whites and Khoikhoi (Hottentots).[1] The first law prohibiting marriage between whites and blacks was introduced in 1685. In Chapter 1 we discussed some of the subsequent measures aimed at preventing blacks from competing with whites and keeping blacks out of white areas.

In this chapter we will consider briefly the most important developments in the twentieth century that contributed to the structure of apartheid. By the time the Nationalists came into power in 1948, apartheid was already thoroughly integrated into the South African political and socioeconomic system. The present government inherited a legacy of race laws, which it subsequently enhanced and refined.

Before 1948, no one pretended that racist laws in any way served the interests of blacks. Colonial and South African governments stated openly their aim of protecting whites, mainly from economic competition, and maintaining a supply of cheap black labor. Only gradually did the fear of political domination by blacks become a factor and social segregation an end in itself. It was not until the 1940s, when Hendrik Verwoerd refined and systematized the policy of apartheid, that the attempt was made to justify race legislation on an ideological basis and to contend that it served the interests of blacks as well as whites.

Lord Milner's Contribution to Racial Conflict

Time began running out rapidly for the hard-won freedom of the Boer republics when the British cabinet decided in 1899 to establish firm control over the whole of Southern Africa. The main thrust of imperialism came from Sir Alfred Milner, British High Commissioner in 1897. He engineered a petition from the Transvaal *uitlanders* (foreigners who were not granted Transvaal citizenship) to the Queen, listing their grievances, especially concerning the franchise, and then used it to provoke a crisis, insisting that "the case for intervention is overwhelming."[2]

Despite the efforts of the Cape government and President Steyn of the Orange Free State to achieve a peaceful settlement, Milner finally had his way. Negotiations broke down, and in October 1899 both sides resorted to force to settle their disagreements. The Orange Free State was automatically drawn into the conflict by a mutual assistance treaty with the Transvaal republic.

The combined republican armies comprised around 60,000 men, of whom never more than 30,000 were in the field at a given time. They were pitted against a British force that eventually numbered almost half a million. Approximately 7,000 British and nearly 4,000 Boers died in the field. A further 30,000 Afrikaners died, mostly in concentration camps, and most of them under sixteen years of age.[3]

Both the war and the Boer republics came to an end with the Peace of Vereeniging in 1902. Lord Milner became High Commissioner of British South Africa and Governor of the Transvaal and Orange River Colonies.

Milner called himself "an imperialist out and out" and a "British race patriot." His main aims were to increase the British population by immigration until the majority of South Africans were English-speaking, and to anglicize South Africa by force, primarily through education. In his Education Ordinance of 1903, he made English the sole language of instruction in state schools. He imported English teachers and made primary education free but voluntary. The Dutch Reformed Church was hostile to Milner's plans and set up the Christelike Nasionale Onderwys, which gave primacy to the Dutch language. Over 200 of these schools were established with no state aid.

Milner vehemently opposed granting political power to blacks. He said: "One of the strongest arguments why the white man must rule is because that is the only possible means of raising the black man, not to our level of civilization—which it is doubtful whether he would ever attain—but to a much higher level than that which he at present occupies."[4] Joseph Chamberlain, head of the colonial office in England, favored enfranchising the blacks so that they might become self-governing. But Milner persuaded him that instead they should be represented in the legislature by whites nominated for this purpose. Article 8 of the Treaty of Vereeniging made the enfranchisement of nonwhites (including Asians and Coloureds) dependent on the consent of a white majority.

A South African Native Affairs Commission appointed by Milner in 1903 to make recommendations to the Transvaal, Orange River, and Cape colonies formalized the idea of racial segregation in a new way: it envisaged the territorial separation of blacks and whites for the purpose of residence and ownership, and approved

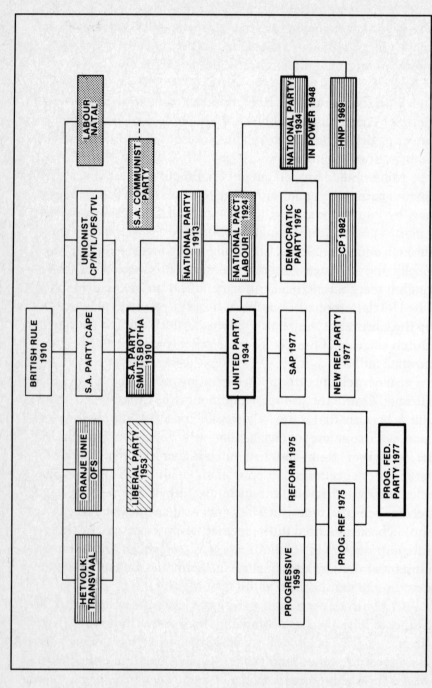

Chart 1   White Political Parties

the establishment of segregated "locations" for urban blacks in various centers. It urged that blacks be represented only by whites in government, and argued for the separation of blacks and whites in political life.

In 1905, Milner was recalled to England and the colonies were granted "self-government." The parties in power at this stage were Het Volk in the Transvaal, Oranje Unie in the Orange River Colony, the South African Party in the Cape, and the Labour Party in Natal.

A National Convention was called in 1908 to decide whether the colonies should form a union or a federation. The government and opposition white parties of the four colonies were represented in almost equal proportions. No blacks, Coloureds, or Asians were present.

In the ensuing debate, Jan Smuts, one of the leaders of Het Volk, argued for a union with uniform race and economic policies. The Natal delegates wanted a federation, believing that this was the only way to protect the rights of the English-speaking minority. The Unionists won the day, but certain policies were left up to the provinces; for example, the question of the franchise for blacks, Coloureds, and Asians. In the Transvaal and Orange River Colony they had no vote, whereas in the Cape and Natal a qualified franchise was retained.

The Union was formed in 1910. In the first election, which took place the same year, Het Volk, the Oranje Unie, and the South African Party joined forces and won a firm majority of seats. The three then united to become the South African Party. Louis Botha, who had been leader of Het Volk, was elected Prime Minister. However, Botha's desire to unite Afrikaans-speaking and English-speaking South Africans soon led to a rift between him and the leader of the former Oranje Unie, J. B. M. Hertzog. Hertzog, an Afrikaner nationalist who wanted Afrikaners to run the country, was finally expelled from the cabinet. He then formed the National Party.

The Native Land Act (No. 27 of 1913)

This legislation was introduced during the first term of the South African Party government and has been discussed briefly in Chapter 1. It forms such an important part of the foundation of apartheid that it must be considered in more detail here.

The bill was a response to numerous complaints the government had received about blacks living in white areas, either on land they owned or rented, or as tenants on white farms. It designated part of South Africa as black territory and prohibited the sale of land in the remaining area to blacks. The area granted to blacks— 10.4 million morgen—comprised only the reserves and locations and was only slightly more than half the area blacks already inhabited. Although intended as a preliminary delimitation, to be reconsidered and increased to more realistic proportions, this was not done until 1936.

Although theoretically the bill applied to all of South Africa, in practice it pertained only to the Transvaal and Natal. The Free State already had legislation prohibiting the sale of land to blacks (Ordinance 5, 1876). In the Cape, property ownership was a qualification for black franchise entrenched in the constitution of the Union, so the Act did not apply.

All the black leaders objected to the Act. The African National Congress sent two deputations to the South African government and one to the British government protesting the bill, but the British were not prepared to intervene. Blacks did not object to the principle of territorial segregation, but to the provisions preventing them from buying land and giving white farmers the right to eject them from land on which they had lived for generations.

The Asians

Asians from the Indian subcontinent were brought into Natal from 1859 onwards as indentured laborers to assist with the sugar industry. After three years they could either buy their freedom for £5 ($60) or remain indentured for another two years. After five years they were free to live and work as they chose, and after ten years they were entitled to passage back to India or to crown land equal to the value of the passage.

Indian traders also came in increasing numbers. The Indian population soon began to create serious competition for whites in trade and agriculture. By 1902, Indians in Natal outnumbered whites.

Considerable pressure was exerted to slow down the influx of Indians, and in 1913 an Immigration Act was passed that, although it did not refer specifically to Indians, made further Indian immigration impossible. Mohandas Gandhi led a protest against the Immigration Act and other laws directed against Indians. As a consequence the Indian Relief Act, which granted some concessions to Indians, was passed.

In 1919 Botha died and Smuts became Prime Minister of the Union. He lacked Botha's personal following, however, and the South African Party began to lose ground to the Nationalists under Hertzog in the rural (Afrikaans-speaking) areas, and to the Labour Party in the urban (English-speaking) areas.

Militant White Trade Unionism

Militant unionism dates from the 1880s and 1890s, when branches of British labor unions were opened in South Africa. One of the leading lights of the labor union movement was an Englishman, W. M. (Bill) Andrews, who later became first secretary of the Communist Party.

The main problem facing white trade unionists was competition from unskilled and skilled black labor. The general secretary of the white workers' labor union blamed "the capitalist class" for this. He explained that, while he was "a Socialist as far as all the workers in the globe are concerned," he believed that his union had the right to fight against and to oust blacks if they were "used [by capitalists] as semi-slaves for the purpose of keeping others down."

What he really objected to, of course, was the beginning of the end of what he called the "semi-slavery . . . of . . . dirty, evil-smelling Kaffirs,"[5] because they threatened the jobs of white miners. These fears came to a head when an economic slump between 1920 and 1923 resulted in the Chamber of Mines proposing a wage cut for whites and an adjustment in the ratios of black and white wages and the number of black and white workers in favor of blacks.

Had the proposals been accepted, many black workers would have been able to enter the mining industry and, in some cases, replace whites, because blacks were prepared to work for £1 per week, compared to the £1 per day that whites demanded.

The white miners found themselves in the somewhat confusing position of fighting on two fronts: on the one hand, against the capitalists and, on the other hand, against black workers. Thus, when they marched through Johannesburg waving red flags, they chanted: "Workers of the world unite and fight for a white South Africa."

In December 1921, the coal mine owners announced a wage cut. On January 1, 1922, the coal miners went on strike, followed ten days later by other white miners.

Feelings ran high against the government, which the striking miners regarded as working hand-in-glove with the owners. In February the miners resolved to overthrow the government and declare a republic. Gangs of white miners roamed the streets committing robbery and arson and attacking blacks. Smuts finally declared martial law. Following fierce street fighting, aircraft bombed the strikers' headquarters.

The rebellion resulted in a great loss of support for Smuts and paved the way for cooperation between the Nationalists and Labour, who agreed to join forces at the next election. Their alliance was based on resentment at the government's alleged disregard for the Afrikaner farmer and the English-speaking white worker and on the mutual esteem of Hertzog and Creswell, leaders of the two parties.

In June 1924 the socialist Labour and Afrikaner National Party Alliance easily unseated the South African Party, and the Pact Government (1924–1933) took over the running of the Union.

Apartheid and Socialism—An Unholy Alliance

The Labour Party members of the Pact Government favored further measures to protect white workers from black competition. The National Party members wanted support programs for farmers and job creation to alleviate the problem of poverty among whites.

General Hertzog, the new Prime Minister, formulated his "civilised labour" policy. "Civilised labour" was defined as "all work done by people whose standard of living conforms to the standard of living generally recognized as decent from a white person's point of view." "Uncivilised labour" he defined as "work performed by persons whose goal is restricted to the mere necessities of life in accordance with the ideas of undeveloped and savage people."[6]

Government departments were instructed to give preference to civilized (white) workers. The fact that blacks were prepared to work for lower wages was to be ignored. One result was that the percentage of whites working for the South African Railways and Harbours (nationalized under Milner) grew from 9.5 percent in 1924 to 28.7 percent in 1929.

In his capacity as Minister of Labour, Creswell incorporated the Civilised Labour policy into the Wages Act of 1925, which introduced a "rate for the job" and minimum wage rates with the specific intention of keeping blacks, Indians, and Coloureds out of certain jobs. No rate was fixed for work that did not interest whites. The Mines and Works Amendment Act of 1926 tightened job reservation on the basis of color (first introduced with the Mines and Works Act of 1911) in the mining industry. Though strongly opposed and rejected in the Senate, the bill was passed by a joint session of the Houses of Parliament.

Creswell was so intent on white worker exclusivity on the mines that he tried an experiment at Village Main mine of having only poor white workers. It was a "deplorable failure."[7]

The Civilised Labour policy also aimed to reinforce the powers of discrimination latent in a number of former Acts. The Factories Act of 1918 enabled the Minister of Labour to withdraw exemptions from customs duties on raw materials if labor conditions were not "satisfactory"—in other words, if nonwhites were being employed when whites were available. The Act also required separate facilities such as toilets, restrooms, and canteens for whites and nonwhites to increase the cost of employing nonwhites. The Apprenticeship Act of 1922 made attendance at technical college compulsory for apprentices. Administered in the spirit of the Civilised Labour policy, it ensured that all better paid jobs were open only to whites.

The Industrial Conciliation Act of 1924, which was ostensibly intended to prevent a recurrence of the violence of the 1922 strike, established industrial councils through which employers and labor unions could negotiate terms of employment. With the approval of the Minister of Labour, such agreements would then acquire the force of law. Whites, Coloureds, and Indians were covered by the

Act, but not blacks. Thus blacks were unable to negotiate at all.

The Labour Party hoped that through these various measures black labor could be excluded permanently from the industrial system. However, "the force of profit-seeking incentives proved more powerful than legislation, and . . . the attempt to segregate the Africans from the modern world and confine them to primitive tribalism in the reserves, or to laboring work on the farms and mines, was far from successful. It barred them only from semi-skilled and skilled employments and not from work classed as unskilled."[8]

The Labour Party also pushed for the nationalization of the iron and steel industry. The more industries the government controlled, the more power it would have to ensure white workers were protected. Again, there was very strong opposition. The bill was blocked twice by the Senate but passed by a joint sitting.

The United Party

In 1933, the National Party under Hertzog and the South African Party under Smuts formed a coalition that won a resounding victory, capturing 136 of the 150 seats in the House of Assembly. The following year the two parties fused to form the United Party. A number of National Party supporters broke away under Dr. D. F. Malan to form the Herenigde Nasionale Party or Volksparty (Reunited National Party).

In 1936, the Representation of Natives Bill was passed by a majority of 168 to 11 in a joint sitting of the two houses, thus abolishing the Cape franchise for blacks. The bill provided for three whites to represent Cape blacks in the House of Assembly.

The Native Trust and Land Act (No. 18 of 1936) added 7.2 million morgen to the land allotted to blacks by the Native Land Act of 1913, increasing it to 13 percent of South Africa's total land area. The Act also exerted further pressure on labor tenants, rent tenants, and sharecroppers on white farms to become wage laborers. It created Labour Tenant Control Boards with the power to terminate voluntary contracts between farmers (mostly Afrikaners) and tenants (mostly blacks).

The Apprenticeship Act (No. 37 of 1944) ensured that standards required for acceptance into an apprenticeship were such that no black would qualify. This Act prevented blacks from entering over 100 trades, and was so effective that by 1974 there were 19,259 white, 331 Coloured, and 426 Indian motor mechanics — but not one black.

The "Swart Gevaar" (Black Threat)

During the years following World War II colonialism became unfashionable, as did the concept of white rule over other races. India and Pakistan gained independence, and in Africa blacks started demanding self-rule. In South Africa, the Native Representative Council, the African National Congress, and the South African Indian Congress began to press for a greater share in government and for the abolition of discriminatory laws.

Whites in South Africa felt increasingly insecure. The United Party policy of permitting racial groups to live side by side with administration and legislation taking their differences into account did nothing to alleviate their fears. The Herenigde Nasionale Party under Malan, in contrast, offered them the continuation of white domination through the concept of separate development. In addition, the Herenigde Nasionale Party appealed strongly to Afrikaner nationalism, and Afrikaners constituted approximately 60 percent of the white population. In the election of May 1948, the Afrikaners came to power.

The Fruition of Apartheid

When the National Party assumed power in 1948 its apartheid policy was certainly not new. Nonetheless, it contained elements that made apartheid before 1948 and apartheid after 1948 somewhat different.

Dr. Malan and his associate, Dr. Verwoerd, decided that the only way to prevent whites, and particularly Afrikaners, from being overwhelmed by blacks and losing their cultural identity was to separate the two races completely. Legislation was therefore aimed at consolidating social, residential, cultural, economic, and political apartheid, with the ultimate goal of ending all interaction between racial groups except on a superficial level in the workplace.

For the first time, an attempt was made to prove that separateness was also in the interest of blacks. It was argued that blacks would be happier and better off governing themselves in their own areas and maintaining racial purity in their ethnic groups.

The Nationalist government implemented apartheid with a ruthless consistency that coincided with increasing world opposition to white supremacy. The new government added the following Acts to the already substantial body of race laws:

Social Apartheid

- The Prohibition of Mixed Marriages Act (No. 55 of 1949) and the Immorality Amendment Act (No. 21 of 1950, Section 16) forbade marriage and extramarital sexual intercourse between whites and blacks, Asians, or Coloureds.

- The Reservation of Separate Amenities Act (No. 49 of 1953) was the primary source of "petty apartheid." It enforced the segregation of elevators, toilets, parks, beaches, hotels, cinemas, restaurants, and so on.

- The Population Registration Act (No. 30 of 1950) provided for a central population register in which all people were classified as whites, Coloureds, or blacks.

Residential Apartheid

- The Group Areas Act (No. 41 of 1950) augmented the laws establishing racially segregated areas. It allowed areas to be proclaimed as belonging to a particular racial group, thereby prohibiting other racial groups from living, trading, or owning land there, and requiring any members of other racial groups already living there to move out. This policy came to be known as "grand apartheid." It meant that, in addition to the black areas already designated under the Native Land Acts of 1913 and 1936, a black "location" had to be provided outside every white urban area and industrial area, with bus or rail transport into the towns and industrial sites.

- This was supplemented by the Natives Resettlement Act (No. 19 of 1954), which was intended to eliminate "black spots" (i.e., black settlements) from white areas. Blacks were moved from white areas and no longer permitted to own their homes. Since the Act, over three million blacks have been forcibly relocated. The Native Laws Amendment Act (No. 54 of 1952) specified that only blacks who were born in urban areas, who had lived there continuously for fifteen years, or who had worked continuously for the same employer for ten years had a right to live permanently in those areas. The Natives (Abolition of Passes and Coordination of Documents) Act (No. 67 of 1952) required all Africans to carry "reference books" with their photographs, places of origin, employment, and records of tax payments and encounters with the police.

- The Natives (Urban Areas) Amendment Act (No. 16 of 1955) aimed at moving blacks out of servants' accommodation in apartment buildings by stipulating that no more than five non-white servants could be accommodated in an apartment building. Subsequent amendments further restricted the movement of urban blacks; these are now known collectively as "influx control."

Cultural Apartheid

- To keep black and white cultures separate, the Bantu Education Act (No. 47 of 1953) and the Extension of University Education Act (No. 45 of 1959) allowed for segregated education. Before this, there was virtually no government education for blacks. Although there was a very effective system of mission schools, these have had to be handed over to the government.

Economic Apartheid

- Existing laws promoting economic apartheid were supplemented by the Native Labour Act (No. 48 of 1953) and the Industrial Conciliation Act (No. 28 of 1956), which segregated trade unions and forbade blacks to strike.

- The Native Trust and Land Act (No. 18 of 1936), now called the Development Trust and Land Act, was supplemented by amendments and proclamations that enabled the government to control every aspect of the black economy, including business, farming, building, townships, land tenure, and tribal authorities. (Some indication of the extent of the Act may be gained from the fact that it stipulates how many times a year buildings must be whitewashed).

- The Natives (Urban Areas) Amendment Act, now called the Black (Urban Areas) Consolidation Act, governs all aspects of black urban living, including business rights, housing, and land allocation.

- Over the years, numerous ordinances, bylaws, regulations, and proclamations were introduced to control licensing. Many of these, although they do not openly discriminate against blacks, achieve "covert apartheid" by setting such high safety, health, and educational standards that blacks are unable to meet them.

- The Physical Planning Act (No. 88 of 1967) forced industry to decentralize to "growth points," "border industry" areas, and homelands. Industries in white areas were not allowed to employ more than three blacks for every one white. This created the current anomaly whereby South Africa has a skilled labor shortage and unemployment simultaneously.

Political Apartheid and the Homeland Policy

- Black representation in white government was abolished and replaced by local boards with a degree of control over local affairs.

- The Asiatic Laws Amendment Act (No. 47 of 1948) abolished Indian representation, since the government regarded Indians as visitors who should return home. In 1964, this policy was reviewed and the South African Indian Council was formed to give Indians a measure of representation.

- The Separate Representation of Voters Act (No. 46 of 1951) removed Cape Coloureds from the white voters' roll and placed them on a separate voters' roll with a Coloured Affairs Council.

- The Bantu Authorities Act (No. 68 of 1951) replaced the Native Representative Council, established in 1936, with a system of Bantu Authorities. This was intended to preserve the cultural traditions and identity of South Africa's various black tribes. It provided for local tribal authorities in the form of traditional chiefs-in-council. The tribal authorities were represented at the regional level, and the regional authorities, in turn, were represented in a single territorial authority for each ethnic group.

- The Promotion of Bantu Self-Government Act (No. 46 of 1959) abolished black representation by whites in the House of Assembly and gave explicit recognition to eight black national units, namely Bophuthatswana for the Tswana, Gazankulu for the Tsonga (or Changaan), KwaZulu for the Zulu, Lebowa for the North Sotho, Qwaqwa for the South Sotho, Venda for the Venda, and Transkei and Ciskei for the two Xhosa tribes. (KwaNdebele for the Ndebele and KaNgwane for the Swazi were established subsequently.)

    These units were established on the land that had already been allocated to blacks, first by the British during the nineteenth century, and subsequently in the Land Acts of 1913 and 1936. This consisted of well over sixty reservations of varying size. Over the years a process of consolidation took place, so that now the ten homelands comprise about twenty separate pieces of land.

- In 1961 the Transkeian Territorial Authority requested self-government for the Transkei. This came about with the promulgation of the Transkei Constitution Act of 1963. This act also provided for Transkeian citizenship. The Bantu Homelands Citizenship Act (No. 26 of 1970) gave all tribal people citizenship in one or another homeland in addition to South Africa.

- In 1971 the Bantu Homelands Constitution Act (No. 21) provided for two phases of constitutional development in the homelands. The second phase allowed considerably more independence than the first, the idea being to encourage the homelands eventually to seek complete independence. It was an important part of the government's policy that the homelands should eventually become fully independent, self-governing states, indistinguishable from Botswana, Swaziland, and Lesotho—the countries created by the British government for the Tswana, Swazi, and Sotho.

- Transkei, Bophuthatswana, Venda, and Ciskei (TBVC) all became independent "national states" between 1976 and 1981. In doing so, all the members of the tribes they represented (who had dual citizenship) lost their right to South African citizenship. This included many people who were not living or working in their allotted homelands, but in "white" South Africa — people who did not qualify for permanent residence under the Native Laws Amendment Act. Citizens of the independent homelands now had to apply for work permits in order to work in South Africa. These were granted only if work was available, and were valid for one-year periods only, so that the individuals concerned would not be able to gain permanent resident status in South Africa. Since the TBVC states continued to employ the restrictive economic practices they inherited, they were unable to provide jobs for their citizens at home. (Ciskei has recently deregulated small business, embarked on a privatization program, and become a tax haven. There has been a net influx of blacks, high employment rates, and healthy economic growth. Some people assume that this has been due to aid from the South African government. But Ciskei receives no more aid than any other homeland government. There are signs that one or two other homelands may follow Ciskei's example. It will be interesting to see whether they achieve the same results.)

In the elections of 1953, 1958, and 1961, support for the National Party increased steadily, largely because the voters were satisfied that apartheid would protect them from economic competition and from black political aspirations. The party became firmly identified with the Afrikaner nation, and thus could count on Afrikaner support, especially after South Africa became a republic in 1961.

Conclusion

In this brief history of South Africa we have attempted to highlight certain factors that are not commonly known, to dispel some myths, and to trace the history that has led to the current impasse.

It is commonly accepted that the Afrikaners are entirely responsible for apartheid and for the current state of massive economic intervention, which we will consider in more detail in the next chapter. However, it is clear from the foregoing pages that, before the Boer War and formation of the Union at the turn of the century, Afrikaners favored limited government and wanted nothing more than a part of the country in which they could live as they wished.

Moreover, when the National Party came to power in 1948, the structure of apartheid was already in place, almost in its totality. All the NP had to do was systematize it. This is not to say the Afrikaners had not been party to racist legislation introduced before that time, but only that all such legislation (apart from laws inherited from the Dutch) was developed jointly with the British colonial government and English-speaking South Africans.

We have also demonstrated the falsity of the idea that the black tribal system is fundamentally socialist. On the contrary, it too is based on individual freedom and private property, which in part explains why blacks responded with such alacrity to market opportunities in the nineteenth century. With new knowledge and the freedom to use it, they became highly successful and enthusiastic entrepreneurs and artisans.

It is primarily these two groups, the Afrikaners and blacks, who must resolve South Africa's future. Many Afrikaners have moved away from their roots, away from their early love of freedom, and now espouse racial socialism or fascism. Similarly, many blacks have moved away from their original belief in individual freedom toward socialism, Marxism, or communism. Both have largely forgotten that decentralization and limited central power were the distinguishing features of their traditional political institutions.

Fortunately, there are many Afrikaners and blacks who are still strongly individualistic, and the future of our country lies in their hands. It is only by returning to their origins, to a system that max-

imizes individual freedom, that blacks, Afrikaners, and all of South
Africa's other groups can live together in peace and prosperity.

PART TWO _____

The Status Quo

> *But man, proud man,*
> *Drest in a little brief authority, . . .*
> *Plays such fantastic tricks*
> *Before high heaven*
> *As make the angels weep.*
> —Shakespeare,
> *Measure for Measure*

Part Two considers the degree of government intervention in the lives of black and white South Africans and the causes of the current political unrest. It also discusses the problems created by redistribution and affirmative action. It concludes with a description of the policies and positions of all the main political parties and pressure groups.

CHAPTER 4

White Capitalism

*That government is best which governs the least, because its
people discipline themselves.*

—Thomas Jefferson

ECONOMIC FACTORS have a powerful effect on the course of events.
Almost every aspect of life — politics, law, education, unemployment,
poverty, unrest — is affected profoundly by economic processes. The
largest issues behind virtually every piece of legislation are economic:
the motives are economic, the means are economic, and the consequences are economic.

When a chain store gives evidence to the government in support of shopping hours legislation; when a manufacturer advocates
minimum standards; when a trade union calls for a certain labor
policy; when a bank supports a particular monetary policy or an
industrialist favors certain tariffs — the measures they propose coincide precisely with their self-interest. But those who call for legislation never admit that they act in their own self-interest. Not one
will say: I believe you should introduce the following law because
it is good for my company, or my business, or the members of my
union, or because it gives me a competitive advantage over others
in my field. Instead, they conceal their real motives under a pretense

of concern for the "public interest," the "national interest," or the "common good."

Cabinet ministers often observe, justifiably, that it is not the government that wants a particular intervention but the private sector. "We were asked by the real estate agents to pass the Estate Agents Act," they say, "so don't blame us. The private sector wanted these laws." Behind every intervention there is a vested interest that benefits from that intervention at the expense of competitors and the general public.

Are White South Africans Free?

It is generally agreed by South Africans of all races, as well as the international community — critics and sympathizers alike — that in our country whites are free and blacks are not. The assumption is that if one simply extends whatever whites have to blacks, blacks will be free. This is not true.

Certainly blacks enjoy far, far less freedom than whites and, equally certainly, they would be very much better off than they are now if they had the same rights as whites. But the economic activity of whites in South Africa is extremely heavily regulated and controlled. If all racially discriminatory legislation were repealed tomorrow, the people of South Africa would still be far from free, and our problems would still be a long way from a satisfactory solution.

The Shackled South African Economy

South Africa is a country of immense, wasted potential. It has the richest endowment of natural resources per capita in the world; it is extremely well-located geographically, with natural harbors, fertile agricultural land, low population density, and easy access to western markets, capital, and technology.

South Africa started industrializing in the late nineteenth century, at the same time as Japan. Yet Japan is an economic giant and South Africa is an economic weakling. Why?

In this chapter, we will attempt to show that the reason we are

lagging so far behind is that our economy has been throttled by policies that would have prevented any country in the world from being
a great economic success, and that these policies have not only
prevented blacks, Indians, and Coloureds from realizing their potential, but have also shackled whites.

Economists posit many different and contradictory precondi-
tions for prosperity: a country needs to be small; it needs to be big;
it needs a homogeneous population; it must have natural resources;
it needs to be near western markets — and so on and so on. But none
of these conditions correlates with what is actually happening around
the world.

Most countries that are well-endowed with natural resources
are economic failures. Successful countries, on the other hand, are
often conspicuously devoid of natural endowment. Many are landlocked, small, and mountainous. Some have no mineral resources,
and they are often heterogeneous. Consider, for example, Switzerland, Singapore, Hong Kong, Britain during the Industrial Revolution, Lichtenstein, Luxembourg, Taiwan, Sri Lanka, South Korea,
Japan, and Iceland. All are economic success stories, while richly
endowed countries such as Angola, Zaire, Zambia, Mexico, Nigeria,
the USSR, North Korea, China, and India perform dismally.

The reason for this apparent anomaly is simple: countries with
free or relatively free markets do well, countries with unfree or
controlled economies do badly. Hong Kong, originally little more
than a rock in the sea, even has to import water. But it has a free
economy. Mexico has vast oil reserves, but the oil industry is nationalized and the country is impoverished.

Guild Socialism

Members of most professions and occupations in South Africa are
protected from competition by means of professional and occupational licensure. In the name of the "public interest," established
members of an occupation or profession ask the government to
empower them to stipulate minimum entry qualifications, to introduce regulations, and to rule that only they may provide certain
services for a fee. These measures enable them to set artificially high

fees for their services with no fear of competition.

Occupational and professional licensing protects not only the competent but also the professionally incompetent. There is a presumption on the part of the public, for example, that someone with a law degree is both competent and qualified. A law student might complete his training without ever having read the Black Urban Areas Act, yet he is entitled to open up offices and offer professional advice to employers and blacks on the Act, and he will not be guilty of fraud or misrepresentation of his professional competence.*

Thus the public loses three times over. First, it is led to believe that every member of a profession or occupation is competent; second, it accepts without question that anyone who purports to have a qualification does in fact have it—there is an assumption that big brother is policing this; and third, by preventing competition, licensure also discourages innovation and improved technology. Because there is no competition, insiders have no incentive to develop more efficient and productive sales methods. We have chosen the legal profession for our example, but the same principles apply in many other closed-shop professions, although some, such as engineering,

---

* At the behest of law societies new lawyers will soon have to have an LL.B. degree despite the fact that some of the lawyers on the Councils do not themselves have an LL.B. They are protected by a "grandfather clause" ensuring that those already in the profession do not need the qualifications they prescribe for their competitors. They get in and slam the door behind them, just as their counterparts in other professions do.

Lawyers argue strenuously that touting or advertising or discounting of legal fees should not be allowed. A lawyer may not say to a poor person, "I will handle your case and charge you only if I win." He may not let it be generally known that he wins 80 percent of his cases and is, therefore, worth consulting. Nor may he advertise that he specializes in consumer or labor protection.

Most lawyers will explain, at great length, the need for the strictest regulations and for a lawyers' monopoly regarding deeds and company registration. They will offer many reasons why only they should be paid for drawing up agreements or wills, although anyone else may do so free of charge. Eminently qualified people such as accountants, bankers, legal advisers, and conveyancers employed by building societies or stockbrokers may not sell or use their legal expertise freely.

In large law firms, conveyancing, debt collecting, and the administration of deceased estates are often handled by "unqualified" paraprofessionals. These individuals have to work for lawyers and may not open specialist practices even though they are manifestly competent to do so. The result is that there is no effective competition in the legal profession, and only a rich man can afford legal advice and services.

are policed by criteria of competence rather than formal qualification. In addition to the professions, there are over 200 licensed
occupations in South Africa. For instance, the sugar industry has
special sugar industry radio communications servicemen, and hyper-
trichologists, who remove unsightly hair, need certain scientific and
aesthetic qualifications in order to do so.

The reason there are so many licensed occupations is that any
small, motivated group — window-cleaners, for example — can ask the
government to pass a law to protect the public from incompetent
window-cleaners (in other words, to protect them from competition).
The effect is precisely the same as that caused by the occupational
guilds of Europe in the Middle Ages: services are kept in short supply,
prices are kept high, and innovation is discouraged.*

Minimum Standards Regulations

In the same way that professional and occupational licensure is
promoted in the name of the public interest, so are minimum standards regulations.

Standards regulations in South Africa tend to be modeled on
First World examples. For instance, when new electrical standards
are introduced by the Federal Trade Commission in the United
States, our bureaucracy in Pretoria hears about them, embellishes
them, and then introduces them with the proud announcement that
we have the highest standards in the world. Because our electrification standards are so high, our electricity is unnecessarily expensive. Consequently, poor people cannot afford it and every winter
old people in low-income areas die because they have no heating.

In the United States, grounding is not required. Investigations
have shown that if it were introduced to save lives (a supposition
that is unproven) it would cost in the region of $10 million per pos-
sible life saved. Many states in the United States do not require that

---

*All that is needed to protect the public from being exploited is an effective application
of the law against fraud. It is fraudulent to purport to have competence and skills one does
not in fact have. If occupational licensure were abolished people would not employ anyone's services without a thorough check or a referral. If they did make a mistake, they could
sue for fraud.

expensive switches be fitted on wall plugs or that wiring be set into walls. But in South Africa, where cheap electricity is so much more important than in the United States, these standards still apply.

For various reasons, health laws have not been enforced in the Operational Area in South West Africa/Namibia for ten years. The benefits for the people living there have been spectacular. Protein-rich foods are much cheaper and more readily available than elsewhere. Fewer children go hungry, malnutrition has decreased, and life expectancy has risen. Small business is booming. There has not been a single recorded incident of illness or disease that health inspectors and health laws would have prevented.

In Ciskei, health regulations are not enforced and "unsafe" food is freely available: unpasteurized milk from unchecked cows and goats, meat and fish that are not shielded from flies, and bread baked in dirty tins are all being sold with impunity. Slaughtering is not regulated and there isn't a single approved slaughterhouse in the country.

What are the consequences? A former Secretary for Health revealed in evidence to the *Louw Commission of Enquiry into the Ciskei Economy* that in fifteen years there had not been one reported incident of disease or food poisoning resulting from unhygienic conditions.

If health laws were applied strictly, the effect would be to double or triple the cost of food. Animals would have to be slaughtered in slaughterhouses costing millions of rands, and regulation butcheries, dairies, and bakeries would cost hundreds of thousands of rands to build and run. The result would be starvation for thousands of Ciskeians who are presently struggling to keep alive.

Health officials enforce regulations because they will be blamed if one child dies from food poisoning or an epidemic. If thousands of children die from malnutrition, however, "rural poverty" is cited as the cause.

There is thus a strong case for repealing health and safety regulations in low-income areas. But what about rich areas? The rich can afford to patronize expensive shops that maintain high standards to attract a wealthy clientele. An alternative to legislated minimum standards would be a voluntary organization that would check standards and award health and quality ratings to shops and manufacturers, in the same way that star ratings are applied to hotels. There are organizations of this nature in several other countries where standards are not controlled by statutory law.

In addition to health and safety regulations that have tragic consequences, there are many thousands of petty rules and regulations that price goods out of the reach of the poor. For example, someone has taken it upon himself to discover precisely what the optimal toilet paper specifications are. The provisions of item 130 in paragraph 2 of regulation 10, schedule 6 to the *Trade Metrology Act* (No. 77 of 1973) govern the "sheet count, ply and sheet size" of toilet paper. In particular, suppliers and retailers "shall sell toilet paper in rolls only when wound around a core having a maximum inner diameter of 40mm. . . ."

Who gains from these regulations? Certainly not the public, many of whom cannot afford regulated toilet paper and are forced to use torn-up newspaper collected from refuse dumps. And certainly not those manufacturers who are willing to enter the market with cheap, "substandard" paper.

Standards regulations produce a multitude of ill effects. They discriminate against small businessmen who cannot afford to enter the market if they have to comply with them. They raise the costs of established businesses so that they have less money for wages, which results in unemployment and lower pay for workers. Consumers are robbed of their freedom to choose from a wide variety of standards and prices. As we have mentioned, most products that comply with standards are priced out of the range of poor people. Minimum standards also discourage innovation, because no one wants to put effort and energy into developing a new product, only to be told it does not comply with standards laid down ten years earlier.

Radical though this may sound, we do not need any compulsory standards regulations. It is unlawful under common law to endanger people's health or safety or to commit fraud, and that is all the protection anyone needs. The new small claims courts are a first step in bringing common law protection within the reach of ordinary people. Over and above that, people should be free to decide for themselves what quality of products to buy.

Agricultural Interventions

There are about twenty-five agricultural control boards in South Africa, including quasi-boards such as the Ko-operatiewe Wijn-bouwers Vereniging (KWV). All of them grant insiders the statutory power to regulate the market to their own advantage. There are many more agricultural regulations that do not involve control boards. For example, there are extensive controls regarding the planting and sell-ing of timber, even though there is no timber control board. A permit is required to plant trees, to cut, process, transport, sell, and export them. It is not clear how all these permits protect the public, but it is very clear how they protect some of the existing plantation and mill owners.

Not only are efficient farmers penalized by a labyrinth of con-trols, but inefficient farmers are supported by a network of subsi-dies at the expense of good farmers and consumers. Farmers who operate at a loss don't go out of business — they receive state subsi-dies. And they are encouraged to overcapitalize because they can write off 100 percent of expenditure on capital equipment against tax in the first year.

Rent Control

Those who favor rent control argue that it protects people who rent accommodation from being exploited by landlords. A few people do benefit by paying low rents, but many more suffer through the shortage of accommodation that rent control causes. Investors will not put money into apartment buildings or townhouses if rent con-trol will prevent them from receiving a competitive return. Also, land-lords are not all wealthy "exploiters," but often ordinary people whose flats or cottages represent all their savings. Rent control prevents them from receiving a fair financial return on their assets.

Price Control

The South African government has performed heroically in the area of price controls. In 1976, there were something like 200,000 con-trolled prices in South Africa; even the Price Controller's Office was unable to keep an accurate count. Now fewer than twenty prices remain under the jurisdiction of the Price Control Act. (There are still many price controls under transport regulations, control boards, and so on.) During the early 1970s people became very creative at finding ways to escape the price controller. In the candy industry, for example, if a Whoozy Bar was controlled at five cents, they would change the shape and package and call it a Woggy Bar, and when a price control was slapped on that, they would bring out a Wiggy Bar. Prices behaved like frogs: as soon as one reached out to catch them, they jumped out of the way, and the price controller never caught up.

Naturally, this was all very wasteful. The real cost of the products was forced up, to the detriment of the consumer whom the controls were supposedly intended to protect. Price controls interfere with the laws of supply and demand, so that controls that fix a maximum price always result in shortages and those that fix a minimum price inevitably create surpluses. This has been amply demonstrated by the agricultural control boards.

"Hidden Apartheid"

All of the regulations we have discussed interfere with private economic transactions between individuals of all races in South Africa. Thus they are not apartheid laws in the overt sense, but they create a kind of "hidden apartheid" of which most people are unaware. Wherever regulations prevent less qualified people from getting jobs or starting businesses, or prevent poor people from buying and selling, the least qualified and the poorest people suffer most. In South Africa, primarily as a result of "black socialism" (which we discuss in the next chapter), the poorest, least qualified people are usually blacks. If the government were to delegislate in these areas, blacks, and to a lesser extent Indians and Coloureds, would be the first to benefit.

State Monopolies

In addition to regulations that interfere with private enterprise, the government controls many other aspects of the economy to the detriment of us all. For example, in South Africa there are both state-owned and state-protected monopolies.

Among the state-owned monopolies, there are the Electricity Supply Commission (ESCOM), the Iron and Steel Corporation (ISCOR), S. A. Transport Services (SATS), Posts and Telecommunications (telephones), and the South African Broadcasting Corporation (SABC). The tentacles of SATS and ISCOR in particular reach out to encompass a wide area of activities. SATS controls railways, airlines, harbors, trucking, and pipelines. These controls are so far-reaching that, for example, no railway line may be built without the consent of Parliament.

South Africans have become so accustomed to government control in these areas that the state monopolies have become sacred cows. Thus, the idea that harbors should be run by private enterprise seems shocking and unimaginable. People trot out the old argument that the private sector cannot afford such big capital projects. But this argument has no basis in reality. Gold mines are more costly than harbors and have longer lead times before becoming profitable, yet they are run very efficiently by private enterprise. Britain has both private and government harbors. The private ports are efficient, have high growth rates, and without any subsidies out-perform the government ones. They are profit-making business ventures. The biggest container harbor in the world is currently being built privately in Hong Kong, and Hong Kong is a smaller economy in every sense than South Africa.

The provision of water by the state is another sacred cow. Of course water must be controlled by the state, people say; it is a public good, a natural monopoly. However, water on the Witwatersrand used to be supplied efficiently by private enterprise. The water supply system in Johannesburg's northern suburbs was installed by a property developer named Frederick Cohen. He bought water from the Rand Mines Water Supply Company and ran a profitable and efficient operation that, after tremendous resistance on his part, was expropriated. The water rates went up and profits turned to losses. At the turn of the century the Rand Mines Water Supply Company was providing water for much of the Witwatersrand. It was nationalized by Lord Milner in 1903 to create the Rand Water Board.

In addition to the state corporations, there are many other parastatals in South Africa, such as the Small Business Development Corporation, the Development Bank of Southern Africa, and the Industrial Development Corporation. Each homeland has one or more development corporations, and the Development Trust owns most of the homeland "consolidation" land and the bus operations in black areas. The agricultural control boards are essentially state marketing and processing corporations with varying degrees of monopoly power.

Labor

In 1984, amendments to the Labour Relations Act of 1956 created a situation in which agreements between employers and trade unions are not enforceable in court unless both the union and the employer organization meet requirements laid down in the original Act. These requirements involve details of constitutions, accounting, office-bearers, and so on. A further amendment extended the Minister's discretion to suspend the operation of agreements, orders, or awards made by arbitrators "in the interests of employers or employees, or in the public or national interest."

Labor relations in South Africa are already a source of major conflict. Greater government involvement simply results in greater politicization and more inter-racial ill-feeling and violence. The government should withdraw from labor matters and allow contracts between employers and employees to be subject to the jurisdiction of the courts only. Nonconsenting parties should not be bound by labor agreements or forced to join employer bodies or unions.

Education

In South Africa, there is "free" and compulsory education for whites but not for blacks. Most people think it is an important priority to provide blacks with the same education as whites. However, since our white education system is one of the least cost-effective in the world, we would question that assumption. Private enterprise can do an excellent job of providing education at all levels, catering for different income groups, different ages, and for a wide variety of needs — ranging from basic literacy to professional training and the teaching of technical skills. At present, the cost of private schools is distorted because all taxpayers must pay for government education whether their children are in government schools or not. The chapter on socioeconomic solutions suggests an alternative to this inefficient system.

Conclusion

There are some 500 acts and numerous ordinances, bylaws, regulations, and policies that inhibit free enterprise in South Africa. Of these, nearly all apply to whites, blacks, Indians, and Coloureds alike. Six acts apply only to Indians, five to Coloureds, and twenty-eight to blacks. Some, like the Group Areas Act, have different effects on each group but apply to all.

If the acts that apply to blacks, Indians, and Coloureds were repealed, the economy would still be severely restricted by the other 450 or more acts. However, whites, and to a lesser extent Indians and Coloureds, still enjoy a degree of free enterprise, whereas the laws that specifically inhibit blacks strike at the heart of their economic freedom. This is why the South African economy is sometimes described as "white capitalism, black socialism." For this reason, we argue in the next chapter that the repeal of laws that prevent blacks from participating in the economy is of the utmost urgency.

CHAPTER 5

Black Socialism

Force, violence, pressure, or compulsion with a view to conformity, is both uncivilized and undemocratic.
— Mahatma Gandhi

IF SOMEONE FROM MARS were told that in South Africa there is a law decreeing that blacks must live in one part of the country and whites in another, he would have no reason, on the face of it, to think that one group was worse off than the other. The Group Areas Act discriminates against blacks, not because it creates separate areas, but because the laws in white and black areas differ. The areas allocated to blacks are much smaller than those allowed to whites, but many places with much higher population densities than our current black areas are extremely prosperous.

If apartheid did no more than separate blacks and whites, Soweto would be a flourishing city with high-rise buildings, banks, department stores, supermarkets, prosperous business people, and numerous entrepreneurs. But it is not. The reason is that blacks live in a socialist world—a world in which almost everything is owned and controlled by the state. This has changed somewhat since certain regulations were relaxed in the 1970s, but essentially we have black socialism in South Africa. There is no genuine private ownership of land or free exchange of land rights in black areas. Government controls the trade unions and the distribution, allocation, and move-ment of labor. Virtually every aspect of life is provided or controlled by government — from houses, hospitals, and day-care centers to schools and transport. It is this that prevents Sowetans from progress-ing, acquiring capital, and becoming entrepreneurs, industrialists, artisans, and professionals.

One of the results of black socialism has been an unholy alli-ance in South Africa between white nationalists and radical socialists, both black and white. Both favor state subsidization and control of blacks; indeed, there is very little difference between their policies for blacks — they just label them differently. Radical white nation-alists say they want to preserve white identity, while socialists say they want to provide blacks with housing, jobs, medical services, education, staple foods, transport, and so on. If Marxists took over the government tomorrow, they would only need to maintain all the current regulations pertaining to blacks and extend them to whites, Indians, and Coloureds as well.

Before 1970

Until the early 1970s, all land in black areas was owned by the state. The Development Trust and Land Act of 1936 made the govern-ment by far the biggest landowner in South Africa. The Act is a draconian piece of legislation, and it is probably still the single greatest source of control over blacks.

Land cannot be used efficiently unless people are free to sell it, mortgage it, lease it, and develop it. To be productive, therefore, it must be privately owned. And the efficient use of land is a neces-sary condition of progress.

Before the late 1970s, no black could open a business in a black urban area unless he had "Section 10" rights. Section 10 of the Black Urban Areas (Consolidation) Act prevented blacks from living in urban areas unless they were born there, had lived there lawfully for fifteen years, or had served with a permit under the same employer in the area for ten years. For those lucky enough to obtain Section 10 rights, there were up to thirty further regulations to contend with before they could start a business. The process of obtaining permission to start a new business could take up to two years and cost thousands of rands. And when all these obstacles were overcome, the applicant would be granted one small site that he could not sell or mortgage and that he had to occupy personally.

One of the few businesses blacks were allowed to run was a general store. No one was allowed to own more than one store, and this could not be bigger than 400 square meters. Such trading stores were granted monopolies under a so-called radius restriction: no two were allowed within three or four kilometers of each other, sometimes eight. Thus even if the monopoly ensured a measure of success, no expansion was allowed. No black could have partners or form a company. Trading was severely curtailed, and industry was banned outright.

There was a handful of successful black businessmen, but so few you could count them on your fingers. Three or four of them made their money on filling station franchises with exclusive monopolies granted before the clampdown on such licenses. That is why Ephraim Tshabalala's filling station in Soweto is said to have done the most business of any in South Africa—no one could get a filling station license nearby.

Other businessmen, like the now famous industrialist Habakuk Shakwane, worked illegally in their backyards, making furniture, fixing cars, and so on, and selling their products as underground black market operators. When various development corporations were established in the 1970s, they sought out underground entrepreneurs to offer them help. Black businessmen describe how on one day, government inspectors were trying to close them down by confiscating their goods and equipment and fining them, while on the following day, other government officials were offering them subsidies and financial assistance to build factories in black development areas.

These few early success stories are important because they testify to the ability of real entrepreneurs to overcome the most extraordinary obstacles. Before the 1980s, the black reserves, locations, and national states probably had less private enterprise than any East European country. There was more economic freedom in Poland, Yugoslavia, Bulgaria, and East Germany than in black South Africa.

After 1970

During the 1970s, many restrictions on blacks were lifted. In 1979, the 99-year leasehold was introduced in black townships. Land could still not be sublet, mortgaged, or sold freely. But leasehold did offer some security of tenure. The Section 10 requirements for businesses were lifted, as were other regulations, and blacks were allowed to register companies and own industries. These reforms resulted in the creation of a substantial black business sector, but they did not put an end to the single greatest source of frustration for blacks — discretionary law.

Discretionary Law

If a white person wants to open a fish and chip shop in a white area, all he has to do is fill out a form, find a zoned business site, and sign a lease with the landlord. If he complies with objectively established health regulations, he is entitled to sell fish and chips. No one must approve of him as a person; no questions are asked about his nationality, competence, resources, or language. No bureaucrat decides if there is adequate "need and desirability" for such a shop. Simply because he is a white in a white area, he is entitled to run a fish and chip shop — or almost any other business or industry.

For a black, the situation is very different. Before he can open a fish and chip shop in Soweto, he has to ask an official for a site. The official may or may not grant his request, for reasons he need not disclose. He may say yes because he likes the applicant, or is related to him, or because he has received a sufficiently generous bribe. He may say no for equally subjective reasons. Once the site has been granted, the potential entrepreneur has to apply to another official for a license. This may or may not be issued, for similar reasons. Then on to the health officials, the building inspectors . . . until, many months and hundreds of rands later, he might be turned down for unspecified reasons.

South African blacks today have no experience of law that applies equally to all regardless of sex, creed, or color. What they experience is arbitrary rule by men, a system that by its nature is rife with both real and suspected corruption. No self-respecting human being can be subjected to such a system without feeling frustrated or angry.

This frustration and anger is vented on apartheid and on "capitalism," which is mistakenly viewed as part and parcel of apartheid. This is particularly ironic because, as we have shown, the source of the frustration is not free enterprise but its opposite: socialism.

Whites say there has been change and reform in South Africa that they can see and feel. Blacks are allowed in places where they were prohibited before; there is black advancement in jobs; blacks share restaurants and theatres and play sports with whites. Opinion polls show a dramatic change in white attitudes. To whites, these changes are substantial, and they cannot understand why blacks keep saying there has been no real change and that all reform to this point has been mere tokenism.

The reason for these divergent perceptions is obvious. Most of the changes affect only the ability of blacks to interact socially with whites, which is relatively unimportant. In their areas, blacks are still subjected to all the same administrative discretions and controls as before. Although they now have freehold title, they still suffer from the bureaucracy, the red tape, the insults; their frustrations remain. There are more opportunities than before, but these too are subject to arbitrary discretion. Where black officials have replaced whites nothing has improved, because the discretionary powers remain the same.

In addition to scrapping influx control (which happened in July of 1986), the government should completely deregulate small business and introduce racial "equivalence" by summarily repealing all laws affecting blacks in black areas that differ from those affecting whites in white areas. Over the years, a massive informal sector has developed in black areas. According to some estimates, by 1980 there were over 800,000 underground businesses, constituting 30 to 40 percent of all economic activity. These will all surge ahead when government gets out of their way.

By removing influx control, deregulating small business, and introducing equivalence, the government would defuse the present critical situation almost overnight, thus giving itself time in which to find an enduring political solution.

Does Apartheid Benefit Whites?

The assumption worldwide is that apartheid benefits whites. It can be easily shown, however, that laws that interfere with voluntary exchange are bad for all South Africans.

Whites do not benefit when they may not develop townships for blacks, rent accommodation to blacks, or trade with blacks. Whites in general do not benefit when blacks are prevented from providing services in white areas; most would favor black bus operators, taxi drivers, traders, shopkeepers, and hotel managers if this meant lower costs and better service. Whites have never benefited from influx control restricting the number of people in black townships. It penalizes whites not only because less labor is available, but also because influx control pushes up the cost of labor, which in turn increases the cost of production and the price of goods to white consumers. And whites do not benefit when they pay for the development policy that creates jobs for blacks in areas where blacks would not otherwise go.

Whites who seek political security have been misled into thinking that they are also gaining economic advantages. We have seen that almost every apartheid law passed before 1948 was aimed at protecting whites from competition. In the short term, these laws did keep some whites employed, and they did prevent some inefficient white farmers and businessmen from going under. But in the long term they benefited no one, and they stopped South Africa from becoming one of the richest countries on earth.

Ethnicity and Achievement

Many white South Africans believe that, by nature, blacks are not achievement-oriented. There are even studies that "prove" that blacks have low motivational and aspirational levels. Whites in South Africa frequently remark that blacks live for the day—they are not interested in saving, investing, or creating wealth.

There is considerable evidence to the contrary. The 1985 World Bank figures place Botswana and Malawi among the top ten countries in the world with regard to growth rates. The Ivory Coast has a prosperous economy and an enterprising, successful, and wealthy black business community. Kenya under Kenyatta achieved consistently high growth rates. Why do these countries succeed, while Ethiopia, Zaire, and Tanzania do not? The reason is that the former countries enjoy economic freedom, and it seems that motivation is directly linked to the opportunities that arise in free markets.*

Most of the homelands in South Africa suffer from the same degree of socialism as the black locations and townships. Consequently, they are notoriously poor and dependent on South African government support.

In Ciskei and, to a lesser extent, Bophuthatswaña, moves have been made to deregulate the economy. Within one year the Ciskeian economy turned around, and Ciskei is now achieving a much higher growth rate than the rest of South Africa.

In Soweto and other townships, the relaxation of the 1970s led to a dramatic increase in the number of successful black entrepreneurs. NAFCOC, the black Chamber of Commerce federation, now has ten thousand paid-up members, which makes it the second-largest business organization in South Africa. There has been an explosion of black entrepreneurs despite the vast assortment of laws that continue to inhibit black business.

Black African countries are not impoverished because blacks run them, but because their economic policies are wrong. Most black South Africans are not frustrated simply because whites rule them, but because they suffer under bureaucracy, red tape, overregulation, and meddlesome officialdom. The real problem is not the color of the people who control the machine, but the nature of the machine. If people have entrenched property rights, freedom of movement,

---

*We predict that, if the aspirational levels of the Chinese in Hong Kong were studied, they would be found to be very high, while those of the Chinese in the People's Republic of China would be very low. Similarly, the aspirations of West Germans would be high, and those of East Germans low. People's aspirations vary with their economic environment and the opportunities it offers them, not with their genetic makeup or cultural background.

exchange, and association; if they are equal before the law and not subject to the whims of officialdom, then racial differences will cease to be so crucial.

This is not to imply that a solution for South Africa should maintain ethnic separation, but to emphasize that separation per se is not what has prevented blacks from advancing. In the course of the last century they have suffered a series of such devastating blows that one can only marvel at the extent to which they have progressed. First they were driven off the land. Then, when they sought employment in the cities, they were denied access to the job market by labor legislation. When they tried to enter business they were stopped by licensing laws, costly minimum standards regulations, and group areas laws. Back in the black reserves and locations they received the final blow: there too the Black Urban Areas Act and the Development Trust and Land Act prevented them from starting businesses or entering industry.

The time has come for all this to change, and for black South Africans to show the world how much they can achieve if free to do so.

CHAPTER 6

Political Unrest:
Causes and Cures

> *Nonviolence is the answer to the crucial political and*
> *moral questions of our time; the need for man to*
> *overcome oppression and violence without resorting to*
> *oppression and violence.*
>
> —Martin Luther King, Jr.

SINCE AUGUST 1984, South Africa has experienced the most prolonged and widespread black civil unrest in its history. Unlike the riots in Sharpeville and Soweto in 1960 and 1976, the current unrest is not confined to major townships but has spread throughout the country, to small locations and townships as well as big ones. It is an expression of widespread black frustration and anger.

Unrest has taken the form of violence and rioting, stay-aways from work and schools, and boycotts of white shops. Individuals who are seen to be connected with "the system" have been targets of violence, mainly in the form of gasoline bomb attacks on their homes.

The trouble began in 1984 when several disturbances preceding the Coloured and Indian parliamentary elections in August culminated in a serious outbreak on the day of the Indian election. In September, rent increases in the Vaal Triangle led to rioting that claimed many lives. Similar waves of violence continued throughout 1985. Since the declaration of a state of emergency in the middle of 1985, the unrest seems to have been only partially contained.

In this chapter, we will consider the underlying causes of the unrest, what can be done to bring it to an end, and why reforms already undertaken have had so little positive effect.

The Economic Recession

The South African economy entered a major recession late in 1981, experienced two consecutive years of declining gross domestic product (GDP) in 1982 and 1983, and enjoyed only a brief upswing from mid-1983 to mid-1984 before resuming the downward trend. The revival that seems to be occurring now has not yet reduced unemployment.

The poor economic performance we have experienced in the 1980s has been largely a consequence of the deteriorating ratio of export prices to import prices and the prolonged drought. But it is perhaps even more a result of rising taxes and an increase in government spending as a proportion of total spending in the economy.

During the past fifteen years, total public sector spending rose alarmingly, from 20 percent of GNP in 1970 to 30 percent in 1985. The ratio of public sector employment to total employment, which had also risen sharply in the 1970s, continued upwards from 20 percent to 30 percent between 1980 and March 1986.

The failure of financial policy was and is the proximate cause of unrest. There are many other causes too, but there is a powerful correlation between unrest and economic decline. People are prepared to accept an imperfect political order indefinitely as long as there is prosperity, growth, and job opportunity. Riots and boycotts tend to occur when people are unemployed and are struggling to make ends meet.

Overregulation

When blacks are asked in surveys what upsets them most about the current system, the factors that rank highest are red tape, long lines, bureaucracy, corruption, harassment, and intimidation. The frustration caused by overregulation is an extremely important contributing factor to the current unrest, as is the hardship and deprivation caused by minimum standards regulations.

Another important aspect of overregulation is politicization. As soon as something is regulated it becomes a political issue. Housing is regulated, so when rents rise the government is blamed and rioting results, as occurred in Sebokeng. Transport is regulated, so when fares rise the government is blamed and buses are stoned and burned, as happened in Mdantsane. Labor is regulated, so labor relations are strained. The political cost to the government of granting the Putco Bus Company a monopoly is immense — and the government gets no compensating benefits. Education is regulated, so when students are unhappy with some aspect of their schooling the government is blamed and rioting ensues.

The following analogy illustrates why overregulation provokes conflict. The production of trousers is an entirely nonpolitical issue at the moment. One never reads in the newspaper that the price of trousers has gone up. Politicians have nothing to say about trousers. Trousers provoke absolutely no political conflict and yet are very important.

We are told that transport, housing, and education are important and that therefore government has to control them. Let us assume that the government, because of the importance of trousers, establishes a Trouser Control Board and a Trouser Development Corporation, and there is a Minister of Trouser Affairs. Trousers would become a source of political conflict and embarrassment for the government. Every time the price of trousers increased, it would result in boycotts, unrest, and unpopularity for the government.

It is ironic that every major wave of unrest in this country has resulted from government controls regarding bus fares, rents, transport, education, and wage rates, none of which were necessary for the maintenance of apartheid.

Unfulfilled Expectations

The South African government's declared policy of change, the announcement by the Minister of Foreign Affairs, Pik Botha, to the United Nations that "apartheid is dead," and promises of political representation for blacks outside the homelands have raised black expectations. These expectations have not been met for various reasons that we consider below.

To most blacks, it seems that only violence produces change. During times of peace and prosperity, reform efforts subside. Then there are the Sharpeville riots, the Soweto riots, the Sebokeng riots, and as a direct consequence, it seems, reform follows. The regulation enforcing Afrikaans as the language of instruction in black schools was the proximate cause of the Soweto riots. The regulation was withdrawn soon after, and apparently as a consequence of, the riots. In reality the government had decided several months before the riots that Afrikaans should not be compulsory, but the decision had not yet been implemented by the bureaucracy.

The Failure of Reform

We have seen that the political cost to the government of controlling and subsidizing the black economy is immense. The government seems to be aware of this and to understand the advantages of deregulation and privatization. A process of reform was set in motion in the 1970s with the introduction of 99-year leasehold, the relaxation of restrictions on black trading rights, relaxations on influx control, the scrapping of job reservation, the legalization of black unions, and the decision to privatize all government-owned houses in the black townships. More recently, the Mixed Marriages Act, the Political Interference Act, and the Immorality Act (Section 16) were repealed; the policy of progressively opening central business districts to all races was introduced; and segregation regarding amenities such as cinemas was relaxed. Influx control was abolished in 1986. The taxi industry was deregulated and health regulations were relaxed in 1987.

If government intervention is indeed the main cause of unrest, why have these reforms had so little effect? Why are they regarded by so many blacks as irrelevant? One reason, which we discussed in the previous chapter, is that the repeal of laws preventing blacks and whites from integrating socially does nothing to mitigate the real frustrations and grievances that result from economic interventions and discretionary law in black areas. But many reforms have involved potentially meaningful and important economic changes, and even these have had little effect. The reason for this is bureaucratic sabotage.

Bureaucratic Sabotage

Bureaucratic sabotage is one of the most serious problems facing South Africa. Many politicians would make a considerable contribution to solving problems if their wishes were actually carried out. Ministers accept their portfolios with grand schemes to deregulate, to get rid of bureaucracy and red tape. They make repeated pronouncements to this effect. But nothing gets done. Every year, for three years in a row, we have heard the Minister of Co-operation and Development announce that there will be open trading areas — but only now have the first few been declared.

When the 99-year leasehold was announced, it was politically quite popular among blacks. That was in 1978. Not until 1985 were leases registered in any significant number. Civil servants simply did not implement the change expeditiously. Why not? Perhaps they were opposed to black home ownership, regardless of what the politicians said, so they dragged their heels; or perhaps they were just hopelessly inefficient. Whatever the reason, when the law was finally implemented, blacks discovered that the leasehold title was a sham. The leases could not be freely traded or mortgaged. The bureaucracy continues to regulate the development, letting, and exchange of land between blacks. Hence there are still virtually no real estate agencies, no newspaper property columns — and, indeed, no property markets — in the townships.

When Dr. Piet Koornhof was Minister of Co-operation and Development in 1980, he asked his officials to draw up three bills to get rid of all "hurtful and unnecessary discrimination." The bills were duly drafted and tabled in Parliament, where, during the second reading, it was realized that the draft bills would have made the situation worse rather than better. Was this a mistake, or was it done deliberately by civil servants who wished to sabotage reform?

The Soweto riots might not have occurred had the government's decision to scrap compulsory Afrikaans been speedily implemented.

The current unrest might similarly have been averted had other political decisions proceeded expeditiously. The bureaucracy simply will not — either because it is inefficient or because it is a law unto itself — expedite politically determined reforms.

How are these problems to be overcome? How can we effectively deregulate and depoliticize society so as to satisfy black expectations?

First, civil servants who disobey orders should be fired, as they would be in the private sector. Second, the government should consider putting deregulation and privatization in the hands of competent and willing private sector agencies that will serve politicians directly, such as the Free Market Foundation, the Law Review Project, and the Privatisation and Local Government Centre.

Power must be devolved from central to local government. Social, racial, ethnic, and economic decisions must be returned to the people they concern, and central government must be confined to aspects of administration that do not provoke conflict. In Part Three of this book we will offer a detailed plan for achieving this end.

CHAPTER 7

The Redistribution of Wealth

The inherent vice of capitalism is the unequal sharing of blessings; the inherent virtue of socialism is the equal sharing of miseries.

—Winston Churchill

MANY BLACKS BELIEVE that, because they have suffered severe disadvantages, any solution to South Africa's problems must begin with a massive redistribution of wealth. The African National Congress (ANC), the Azanian People's Organisation (AZAPO), the National Forum (NF), and the United Democratic Front (UDF) all favor some degree of wealth redistribution.

The analogy of a race helps explain their perception. In this race, blacks have been held at the starting line while whites run halfway around the track. Now blacks are being told that they can join the race—but from their current position well behind whites. Understandably, they feel this is unfair. Whites should come back to the start, so that blacks and whites can begin again closer to each other.

It is easy to sympathize with this view. Blacks have been subjected to gross injustices. If these could be redressed simply by redistributing wealth, we would have a quick and easy solution to our problems. But all the evidence we have shows that redistribution doesn't help the people it is intended to help as much as it is supposed to. The poor are not made prosperous by impoverishing the rich.

In this chapter, we will examine the contention that taking wealth from the rich in South Africa and giving it to the poor will benefit the poor substantially and permanently. We will discuss the negative consequences of redistribution, as well as the practical difficulties involved in implementing it. And we will offer a suggestion for compensating blacks in a way that would benefit the economy, and hence the prospect of prosperity for all South Africans.

Economic Misconceptions

The Zero Sum Fallacy.   According to the zero sum theory of exchange, one person's gain is another person's loss. In the words of John Ruskin, "Whenever material gain follows exchange, for every plus there is a precisely equal minus."

If this is true, then whenever a profit is made, it is made at the expense of another person. But it is not true. On the contrary, both parties gain from voluntary exchange.

Professor Carl Bauer, head of the Economics Department at Fort Hare University, uses a simple analogy to demonstrate this. Two boys meet in the street. One plays rugby and the other soccer. The rugby player has a soccer ball and the soccer player has a rugby ball, and they agree to exchange balls. Everyone will agree that now they are both better off, yet neither has incurred a loss. There is still only one soccer ball and one rugby ball, but there has been a gain. Similarly, when Pick 'n Pay stores sell goods at lower prices than other supermarkets, their customers benefit and more people want to buy from them. If their business increases, they make bigger profits and are able to open more stores so that even more people may benefit from their low prices. When an employer offers someone a job and the job is accepted, both the employee and the employer gain: they are both better off than they were.

This is true of every free exchange, because people would not agree to an exchange if, in their own view, they did not gain from it. Sometimes they make a mistake, but this doesn't alter the principle. The only time mutual gain does not occur is when laws are passed that interfere with free exchange.

The zero sum theory implies that if blacks suffer disadvantages, whites automatically benefit; conversely, if blacks benefit, whites inevitably lose. In truth, in a free society every exchange between blacks and whites would be to their mutual gain. Clearly, a white landlord is better off if he is allowed to lease or sell property to blacks, and a black restaurateur benefits if he can serve whites.

In South Africa, as we have seen, many laws have been passed that interfere with free exchange, especially with black freedom of exchange. It is these *laws* that have held blacks back, not white advantages.

The Rich Get Richer and the Poor Get Poorer. One corollary of the zero sum fallacy is the conclusion that, as the rich get richer, the poor get poorer. Various studies undertaken in South Africa, however, and in particular a research project on white and black incomes undertaken by the Department of Economics at the University of Natal, present compelling evidence to the contrary.[1]

Consider these figures: Between 1917 and 1970, black and white shares of national income remained remarkably constant. White income averaged 73.5 percent of the total, while blacks, Indians, and Coloureds shared the remaining 26.5 percent, with blacks averaging 17 percent of the total. After 1970 a dramatic change occurred. In five years, the black, Indian, and Coloured share of income grew from 26 percent to 32 percent and the white share dropped from 74 percent to 68 percent. By 1980, the black, Indian, and Coloured share had risen to approximately 40 percent of the total.

The gains made by blacks, Indians, and Coloureds were not made at the expense of whites, however. South Africa experienced its highest growth rates during the early 1970s. In other words, while the black share of the cake was increasing, the cake itself was increasing at an impressive rate, so that blacks were getting a bigger share of a bigger cake. Whites were getting a smaller share of a bigger cake, but their slice was nonetheless considerably bigger than before. A

study by the Bureau of Market Research of the University of South
Africa showed that, between 1960 and 1980, the real personal income
of all South Africans (excluding the independent homelands) rose
by 115.2 percent. White incomes rose by 112.1 percent, black incomes
by 220.8 percent, Coloured incomes by 246.6 percent, and Indian
incomes by 332.5 percent.

What brought about this sudden change? Before 1970, there
was massive wealth redistribution from whites to blacks and, simultaneously, severe restrictions on black economic activity. After 1970,
there was a net relaxation of restrictions on blacks, which produced
a rapid increase in black upward mobility. Redistribution thus failed
to improve the lot of blacks, whereas a very small measure of black
participation in the market achieved remarkable results. The rise
in black incomes was linked to large wage increases in the mining
industry when the price of gold rose rapidly in the early 1970s, but
perhaps had even more to do with a substantial growth in the number of black professionals, technicians, managers, administrators,
clerks, and salespeople. The annual growth rates for the six-year
period 1969–1975 were:

	Whites	Coloureds	Asians	Blacks
Professional & Technical	7.7%	8.9%	10.6%	15.4%
Managerial & Administrative	9.8%	28.8%	17.6%	44.7%
Clerical	4.9%	14.1%	16.9%	15.1%
Sales	5.7%	20.7%	12.1%	6.8%

The Onerous Cost of Black Socialism

In the course of South Africa's history, a staggering amount of wealth
has been transferred from whites to blacks. South Africa has one
of the most severely progressive tax systems in the world. Sweden
is generally regarded as redistributing more wealth than any other
country, but South Africa is not far behind. Maximum personal
income tax in Sweden is 57 percent, in South Africa about 50 percent. Maximum company tax in Sweden is 40 percent of profits, in
South Africa 50 percent.

Although it is difficult to assess precisely who bears the final tax burden, the bulk of direct tax is paid by whites. Taking all forms of taxation into account, it is estimated that at least 75 percent of national tax is paid by whites, and probably more. Whites pay about 90 percent of income tax and an even higher percentage of company tax. Much of this money pays for black socialism and apartheid. Whites pay for black housing, transport, and schools as well as homeland development, food subsidies, separate amenities, and necessary incidentals such as international propaganda and ideological censorship.

Dr. Frederik van Zyl Slabbert, former leader of the Progressive Federal Party, observed in Parliament that the government has paid R1.6 billion per annum directly to the homelands in addition to the R627 million they receive indirectly. This expenditure has succeeded in increasing the real per capita gross domestic product (GDP) in the homelands from R40 to only R46 between 1970 and 1980. In the tax year 1984–85, the homelands were paid a combined total of R2.2 billion — 8.8 percent of the budget.

We have talked about the rape of black land that occurred throughout South Africa's history, but many whites have been driven from their land too. Thousands of white farms have been expropriated for incorporation into homelands, locations, or the Development Trust. Many more thousands have lost their homes, along with blacks, Indians, and Coloureds, as various residential areas have been reallocated from one group to another.*

Both government and homeland officials have made the disastrous mistake of confusing ownership and jurisdiction. In other words, they have assumed that if a boundary is moved all the land affected must be expropriated. As a consequence, entire white towns such as Port St. Johns and Seymour have been expropriated for incorporation into black areas, when boundaries could simply have been moved so that the towns would fall under a new jurisdiction. When farms, shops, hotels, and businesses are expropriated, all goodwill,

---

*A classic case of "musical township" occurred when whites were moved out of parts of Mayfair in Johannesburg so that it could become an Indian area, while simultaneously Indians in Pageview/Vrededrop, just down the road, were evicted so that their area could become white.

Diagramatic representation of high and low income gradients

On the base line of the triangles are those who earn the least. At the apex are those who earn the most.

A illustrates and economy with a high income gradient: relatively few poor people; lots of upward mobility; high expectations.
Dotted △ shows potential income distribution.

B illustrates an economy with a low income gradient: many poor people; little upward mobility; low expectations.

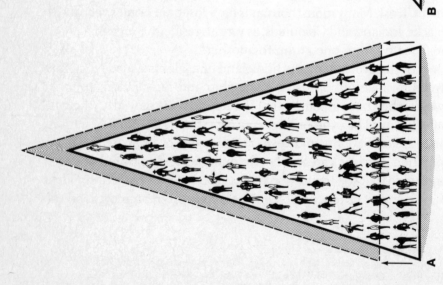

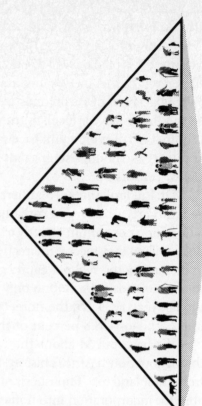

Figure 1   Income Gradients

expertise, energy, and capital invested by their erstwhile owners are lost. None of this waste need occur.

Income Gradients

Mathematicians and econometricians have made some interesting discoveries about income gradients that refute the view that, if all incomes are roughly equal, most people will benefit.

In grossly simplified terms, an income gradient is the measurement of the ratio of high income to low income earners in a society. The greater the difference between high and low incomes in a country, corporation, or business, the higher the income gradient.

An examination of the income gradients in various countries shows that gradients exceeding 0.6 correlate with prosperity. In fact, the higher the gradient, the greater the prosperity of the country as experienced by the average citizen (see Fig. 1).

During the nineteenth century, when income tax rates were negligible, gradients were usually between 0.58 and 0.78. In the twentieth century, as taxation increased, income gradients began to fall. A few years ago South Africa had the lowest gradient in the world, at 0.33. It has now risen to 0.4, more or less the same as the United Kingdom. South Africa's heavily progressive tax system, combined with black socialism, is the primary reason for this inordinately low income gradient.

Income gradients vary across different sectors of the economy. In sectors with high gradients, there is high upward mobility. People are motivated to work by the potential for advancement. This upward mobility affects the entire sector so that ultimately the lowest incomes are higher than those in sectors with low gradients. Not surprisingly, sectors with low gradients lose personnel regularly as people migrate to greener pastures where income gradients are higher.

K. A. H. Adams, one of the world's experts on income gradients, concludes that, if steps are taken to improve conditions by equalizing incomes, conditions will in fact worsen. Instead, marginal tax rates should be reduced to a maximum of 33⅓ percent, which will result in steeper gradients and rapidly increased growth rates. The fiscal loss would be quickly made up by increased productivity.[2]

Practical Difficulties with Redistribution

It is very easy to talk about redistributing wealth, and superficially the idea has obvious attractions. In reality, a host of problems arise.

It is virtually impossible to determine which blacks should be compensated and to what extent — and which whites should pay the cost. There is no way of knowing who has suffered most and who is most to blame.

Nor is it easy to decide what should be redistributed. We have mentioned that our tax system is already so severely progressive that it retards economic growth and penalizes whites and blacks alike. If white property is to be shared out, the question is, how? If all white cars, homes, and farms were dumped on the market, their prices would drop precipitously and revenues would be much lower than expected. Everyone would be a net loser. Alternatively, if cars and houses belonging to whites were given to a few black families, as happened in Transkei and other areas, the vast majority of blacks would be no better off. In the process, most whites with skills, quali-fications, and productive potential would leave the country. Many would go out of business. And there would be massive distortions and malinvestment throughout the country.

If white farmland were divided into small plots and parceled out to blacks there would be the same disastrous results through-out the country that this policy caused in the homelands, which we discussed in Chapter 1 as a major cause of the downfall of blacks. If the new landowners were free to lease or sell the land, it would rapidly find its way back into the hands of the best farmers, who for the present are mostly whites. If they were allowed to dispose of the land only to other blacks, it would gravitate into the hands of the best black farmers, of whom there are presently only a hand-ful with the same proven competence as whites. This would lead to an even greater concentration of land in the hands of a smaller elite than at present.

If the intention is to redistribute wealth by transferring assets to the government on behalf of "the people," we must repeat that massive redistributions have already occurred. Billions of rands have been transferred to black homeland governments from whites. Most of this money supports bureaucratic structures. "The people" do not benefit. In addition, all the assets presently owned by the South African government—state corporations, black townships, vast expanses of land, beaches, harbors, roads, buildings—belong to "the people." If the government consisted of black instead of white people, it would not make an iota of difference.

If wealth is to be redistributed in the form of welfare, the inefficiency of doing so should be kept in mind. Statistics for the United States show that, while welfare spending is calculated at around $48,000 per family of four, each poor family receives only between $6,500 and $8,000 worth of welfare. The rest is swallowed up by administration.[3]

The frustrating truth is that redistribution is very difficult to achieve. In the past, attempts to redistribute wealth have invariably resulted in a redistribution of poverty. In Africa, this has been true of every attempt to transfer wealth from the rich to the poor. In Zaire, President Mobuto Sese Seko nationalized all private assets so that white wealth could be enjoyed by blacks. When the economy collapsed, he invited the dispossessed businessmen, farmers, and industrialists back, but his invitation was declined. In contrast, in Zimbabwe, the Mugabe government promised redistribution but soon found that the consequences of any move in that direction were disastrous. As a result, whites' assets have by and large been left alone, and black disadvantages are being offset by greater access to opportunities previously reserved for whites. Zimbabwe's economy is performing fairly well, while Zaire is virtually bankrupt.

Compensation Is Possible

We have argued that the economic theory behind redistribution is fundamentally flawed and that, in practice, transfers of wealth from rich to poor result in a net loss for everyone.

Nonetheless, for 300 years South African blacks, and to a lesser degree Indians and Coloureds, have suffered gross violations of their rights. Their anger is entirely justified. The damage that has been done cannot be accurately calculated, nor can it be adequately redressed. But it is possible for white South Africans to offer some compensation as a gesture of contrition.

The government's share of the country's wealth has grown throughout this century so that now, directly or indirectly, it accounts for almost half of new capital formation and one-third of all economic activity. If government assets were privatized, vast amounts of money would be mobilized for compensation. At the same time, the economy would receive a tremendous boost.

If government assets were put on the market, most of the buyers would be white, because whites own most of the wealth. The money raised in this way could be used to establish a fund from which compensation could be paid to blacks. Everyone would gain: new investment opportunities would be created; the economy would benefit enormously because private enterprise is so much more efficient than government enterprise; and blacks would receive a capital sum to invest or to use for short-term needs.

This method of redistribution would require little or no economic disruption, and would reduce malinvestment substantially. It would be popular among whites, even though the wealthiest whites would foot the bill. It would also attract much-needed foreign investment.

Who Should Qualify for Compensation?   Some may believe that only adult blacks should be compensated. Others may argue that present disadvantages will affect future generations. A practical compromise might be that all blacks born before the year in which apartheid is abolished, say 1989, will be entitled to compensation; monies owing to children would be held in trust by their guardians until they reach the age of majority. Whether Indians and Coloureds should receive the same compensation as blacks or less would have to be considered.

How Much Compensation Should Be Paid?   The amount of compensation would also have to be based on practical considerations. A starting point would be the potential income from privatization of government assets, divided by the number of people qualifying.

Administration of Compensation.   This should be done through established financial institutions such as banks and building societies in order to prevent the kind of bureaucratic waste and obstruction mentioned earlier. Financial institutions have the machinery and expertise to handle the issuing, cashing, and transfer of redistribution payments. They also have branches throughout the country that are accessible to most people. Interest would automatically accrue on unclaimed amounts.

That the market is able to mobilize enough capital to privatize vast state assets was demonstrated unambiguously by the public flotation of Sasol's shares, which were subscribed twenty times over. Presumably, privatization would occur over a number of years. The proceeds would go into a fund out of which fixed amounts could be paid at regular intervals, or dividends could be declared from time to time as resources become available.

Conclusion

We have suggested a method for paying compensation without excessive disruption of the economy. In the long run, though, the unrestricted mobility of people and resources is much more important to blacks than compensation. Throughout the world, over and over again, we have seen that free markets lift people out of poverty far more rapidly than any other economic system known to man.

Underlying all the arguments for the equal distribution of wealth and income is the implication that no one should have more or less than the next person. The Glen Grey Act of 1894, which we discussed in the first chapter of this book, was based on this principle: it decreed that no black man could buy more than one piece of land, so that no man could become richer than another.

The response of Charles Pamla, spokesman for the black commercial farmers, to this law bears repeating:

> This shuts out all improvements and industry of some individuals who may work and buy. . . . Surely Mr. Rhodes can't expect that all natives will be equal. He himself is richer than others; even trees differ in height.

Black South Africans have been manacled by socialism for over a century. Now is the time to break those chains, not to strengthen them.

CHAPTER 8

Affirmative Action

*My race need no special defense, for the past history of them
in this country proves them to be the equal of any people
anywhere. All they need is an equal chance in the battle of life.*
— Robert Smalls (Black U.S. Congressman 1874–1886)

IF YOU ASK THE AVERAGE PERSON whether people should be free
to mix with one another or not, as they choose, the answer will nearly
always be yes. Yet many of those who strongly oppose apartheid are
now calling for a new kind of racial intervention — affirmative action.

Affirmative action takes many forms, and the intentions behind
the laws are usually good. Unfortunately, the outcomes are often
the opposite of what was intended.

Negative Economic Effects

In the United States black incomes are substantially lower on average than white incomes. During the 1950s and 1960s, the gap
between the two began to close, and the black share of the GNP
increased. If these gains had continued at the same rate, it was calculated, young educated blacks entering the labor force in the year
2000 would be earning as much as whites. But the growth of the
1960s was slowed during the 1970s by the affirmative action laws
enacted during the civil rights era. Many of the anti-discrimination
laws introduced to help blacks hindered them instead.

For both objective and subjective reasons certain categories of people are less in demand in the labor market than others. Among these are people who lack skills or education, teenagers, the elderly, blacks, women, and immigrants. Skilled white men find jobs most easily.

Blacks, women, and other less sought-after groups can compete with white men only by offering to work for less. Once they have jobs they can prove their worth and demand higher wages. But equal pay and minimum wage laws prevent such people from undercutting their competitors in this way. Often, the people who lobby for laws "to protect workers from exploitation" are the insiders who don't want competition.

It is well known that equal pay and minimum wage laws discourage employers from hiring less sought-after people, so quota laws and wrongful dismissal laws are introduced to counteract this effect. These laws force employers to hire a given number of blacks and women, and prevent them from dismissing anyone without good reason. Unfortunately, this sometimes has the effect of aggravating prejudices and of making employers less inclined than ever to employ protected people.

Unskilled workers suffer most under affirmative action. In 1948, black teenagers aged 16 and 17 had an unemployment rate of 9.4 percent, while the rate for whites in the same age group was 10.2 percent. Now white teenage unemployment is around 17 percent, but black teenage unemployment has soared to 40 percent and, in some cities, as high as 70 percent.[1] This is a direct result of affirmative action laws combined with minimum wage laws, occupational licensing laws, and apprenticeship laws, which block entry into the market.

Freedom to Disassociate

The freedom to disassociate is just as important a part of individual liberty as the freedom to associate. In South Africa, children are prevented, solely on account of their skin color, from sitting next to each other in school. In the U. S. children are forced, solely on account of their skin color, to sit next to each other in school. They are bused, sometimes one or two hours each way, to and from school, so that black and white children will receive the same education, regardless of its standard or of what they or their parents want.

One of the little-known negative consequences of racial integration policy has been the destruction of a number of very successful black schools. Thomas Sowell, a prominent black American economist, cites the example of Dunbar High School in Washington, D.C. This all-black school had an impressive record during its first eighty-five years: the first black general in the United States, the first black cabinet member, the first black federal judge, the first black professor at a national university and the discoverer of blood plasma — all were graduates of Dunbar High School. At the turn of the century, its students scored higher on tests than students from any white school in Washington. This school was destroyed in two to three years by forced racial integration; its high academic standards disappeared entirely.

The Market Is Colorblind

Overwhelmingly, people freely choose not to discriminate in business or employment because, if they do discriminate, their business will inevitably suffer. This is why apartheid laws were introduced — to stop people who wanted to do so from mixing and trading with other races.

If one cafe owner chooses not to serve blacks, it won't be long before another trader will see the gap in the market and fill it. The new shop will soon out-compete the other unless the first one has sufficient nonblack support to keep going.

If a factory owner refuses to employ black labor, he will have to pay a higher price for white labor. Provided the market is free, someone will see the opportunity to undercut him by employing black labor and cutting costs. The factory owner who discriminates will be driven out of the market or forced to employ unskilled labor himself. As black labor becomes scarcer, the demand for it will increase and wages will rise in response to this demand.

Only where there is a high demand for a segregated facility will it withstand competition from integrated facilities and survive in the marketplace. The entire weight of apartheid has not been sufficient to stop shops, restaurants, and theaters from catering to all racial groups in response to economic pressure.

The "Bittereinders"

There are a number of white and black nationalists in South Africa who do not want to mix with members of other races. Some whites will fight to the bitter end for the right to buy land and establish white areas through private ownership. This should be recognized as a legitimate way of meeting their needs.

Birds of a Feather

Laws are introduced to stop people from doing things they otherwise might do. If laws are necessary to force people to integrate, it is because there are many people who prefer not to.

Evidence that this is so is found in every heterogeneous country in the world. In New York City, the degree of racial segregation in parts of the city is as rigid as anything ever dreamed of in South Africa. Whites are not welcome there, and they don't go there. No amount of affirmative action can change this. Various Chinese communities in American cities are extremely segregated and highly conscious of their ethnicity. There are culturally and ethnically exclusive residential areas all over the world, and this kind of separation usually does not cause offense because it is voluntary.

When apartheid laws were abolished in South West Africa/ Namibia and Zimbabwe, there was no "melting pot" effect. A few blacks moved into white areas and vice versa, but on the whole people stayed where they were. But racial insult was removed, dignity was restored, and hostility has reduced.

Conclusion

In a free society, people are forced neither together nor apart. Left alone, people all over the world integrate and segregate spontaneously and to the overwhelming satisfaction of most of them. As soon as governments interfere with the right of individuals to make such choices, they cause serious problems. In a country like South Africa, with many different groups representing many different value systems, it is particularly important to cultivate a tolerance for diversity.

CHAPTER 9

The Political Status Quo

The difference between politics and statesmanship is philosophy.

—Will and Ariel Durant

WHAT ARE THE MAJOR political groupings in South Africa? Where do they fit into the scheme of things? What are their positions and how do they differ from each other? How representative are they? And how, ultimately, would they fit into a solution to South Africa's problems? These are the questions addressed in this chapter.

The False Left-Right Dichotomy

The political distinction between "left" and "right" is always dangerous and misleading. First, it implies that there are only two political and economic options, whereas in reality there are many. Second, it is based on the assumption that "left" and "right" positions are at opposite ends of the political spectrum, whereas in truth the groups that the terms popularly describe have a great deal in common with each other.

Typically, the left is identified with an economic order in which the state owns the means of production and controls economic activity, supposedly on behalf of "the people." The right is identified

with a system in which the means of production are privately owned
and economic activity is constrained only by the conditions found
in free markets.

This inadequate and misleading dualistic analysis is rendered
even more confusing in South Africa than elsewhere by the fact that
"left" and "right" usually refer specifically to one's position regarding race policy. Thus, even if you are a radical laissez-faire propo-
nent, if you are opposed to apartheid, you are considered left-wing.

Conversely, even if you approve of full-fledged nationalization,
welfare statism, unbridled state control, central planning, and all the
other trappings of socialism, if you favor apartheid you will be called
right-wing. The advocates of apartheid and socialism regard the two
dogmas as opposites, even though "social engineering" is central
to both.

"Left" and "right" in South Africa have little to do with one's
position on nuclear energy, civil liberties, economic policy, foreign
policy, environmental policy, welfare, trade unions, or education.
In fact, such matters scarcely figure in the South African debate;
only the active members of a party who read its literature and attend
its congresses have any idea of its policy on these issues.

If you were to ask well-informed South Africans—political
journalists or academics, for example—about National Party constitutional policy, New Republic Party policy on control boards,
Progressive Federal Party policy on pollution or environmentalism,
or African National Congress policy on trading hours, the chances
are they would not know. But they would have a good idea of every
party's position on the race issue. Inquiries reveal that in truth none
of the political groups except the National Party has established
positions on most other issues. Racial politics is all-absorbing. Left-
right analysis, therefore, in no way contributes to an understanding
of South Africa's political groupings.

The political groups discussed in this chapter include political
parties, politicized labor, and other pressure groups. They are presented in alphabetical order, rather than by size or prominence,
because popular support is impossible to determine for many groups
and because there is almost no correlation between the prominence
of a group and the number of people it represents.

The actual membership of each of the major groupings is surprisingly small—and that includes even the prominent white political parties as a percentage of the white electorate. People are no
longer blindly committed to particular groupings and there is a large
floating vote. Moreover, during the 1950s and 1960s, there was a much
clearer delineation between the United Party and the National Party,
the Pan-Africanist Congress (PAC) and the ANC, and so on. Now
numerous splinter groups have cropped up in between the major
parties and it is difficult to establish the precise position of any group
regarding South Africa's future.

Political Parties and Pressure Groups

African National Congress (ANC).   The ANC is a largely black
political grouping formed in 1912 and banned in 1960. The ANC's
aim, as set out in the Freedom Charter, which was formulated at
the Congress of the People in 1955, is to turn South Africa into a
social democracy. Its leader, Nelson Mandela, was convicted of con-
spiring to commit treason and sabotage and was imprisoned on Robben
Island under a life sentence. The ANC re-formed itself in South
Africa's neighboring countries under the leadership of Oliver Tambo.
     Until 1969, the ANC officially followed a policy of nonviolence
in its effort to bring about an end to apartheid. At the Morogoro
Conference in that year, the ANC approved a policy of violence
against the South African government. During the 1970s, it went
through a period of political and military consolidation accelerated
by the arrival of some 9,000 black refugees from South Africa after
the Soweto riots in 1976. It is difficult to assess the number of ANC
sympathizers with any accuracy, but it is safe to say that the organization has one of the biggest followings among black South Africans.
     In a sense, the ANC has internal apartheid. It is multiracial
rather than nonracial and has associated members from nonblack
groups represented in the Coloured People's Congress, the regional
Indian Congresses, the Congress of Democrats for whites, and the
South African Congress of Trade Unions (SACTU), which comprises
"working class" people from all races. These groups are united under
the Congress Alliance.

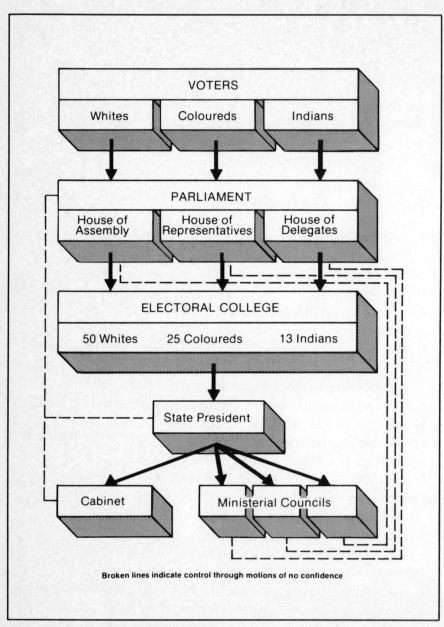

Chart 2 Present Tricameral Parliament

The Freedom Charter envisages a future for South Africa in which the rights of different national groups are protected and all groups have equal status. Some kind of power-sharing is envisaged, and certainly a degree of wealth redistribution, especially of land. The Charter is important, as it represents the first formal expression of the aspirations of a group possibly representing the majority in South Africa. Although it means different things to different people and contains sweeping generalizations that are highly ambiguous and open to widely varying interpretations, this may prove to be a good thing.

The Charter includes the following aims: All "national [race] groups" should have equal rights. Land should be shared among those who work it. There will be work and security for all, houses and comfort for all, and peace and friendship. There will be private land ownership, and most of commerce and industry will be private. The Charter would nationalize mineral wealth, banks, and industrial monopolies.

Some political groups would like to push the ANC toward a more radical socialist position. One of these is the Communist Party. After the party was banned in the 1950s, South African communists decided to support the Congress Alliance. But they regard the ANC goal of social democracy as only the first stage in the transformation of South African society. The Communist Party envisages a second stage in which a socialist revolution occurs and the working class comes to power. At that point the state will assume ownership of and control all the means of production and distribution.

It should be noted that the ANC was willing to talk to the government prior to its banning in 1960. Only then did it embark on its policy of confrontation. The government should lift the ban and release Nelson Mandela if it wishes to negotiate a settlement with all representative groups in the country.

Azanian People's Organisation (AZAPO). AZAPO was formed in 1978 out of the ruins of various black consciousness groups broken up after a clampdown in 1977. By early 1984 the organization had 93 branches in twelve regions, and 1,547 delegates and observers attended its annual congress.

AZAPO is fundamentally a black group. Some members would like to exclude whites from its ranks, while others are prepared to accept some on an individual basis on the understanding that they work in white communities preparing their fellow whites for change. AZAPO is anti-capitalist, anti-liberal, and anti-foreign interference. It is not interested in talking to the government or in cooperating in any way. It sees the government's desire for dialogue as a move to compromise liberation movements.

AZAPO's aim is to achieve black majority rule in a socialist state and to nationalize all means of production, all productive land, all means of communication, and all banks and insurance companies. It is affiliated to the National Forum, and its members experience considerable harassment by the security police.

Afrikanerweerstandsbeweging (AWB) (Afrikaner Resistance Movement). The AWB was formed in 1973. Its members are Afrikaner nationalists who operate outside the political party system and advocate rigid ethnic separation in South Africa.

The AWB maintains that its leader, Eugene Terre' Blanche, speaks to at least 1,000 people a week and that cassettes of his speeches have been borrowed 100,000 times. It is not prepared to give membership numbers for "strategic reasons." Among its sympathizers are supporters of a cross section of Afrikaner nationalist political parties.

The AWB advocates a Boer republic for the *Boerevolk*. The area it wants for this is rather large, comprising a good third of the country and including the entire Transvaal and Free State. It would like to see South Africa divided into *vrye volkstate* based not on color but on history, tradition, language, and culture. In other words, it would split both whites and blacks into separate cultural groups. Each *volk* would have its own leaders within its own geographical area. The electorate of the *Boerevolkstaat* would consist only of Afrikaners.

Conservative Party (CP). The Conservative Party was formed in 1982 by a group breaking away from the ruling National Party in protest against its policy of change. The party leader is Dr. Andries Treurnicht, and its official newsletter, *Patriot*, has 17,000 subscribers.

The CP would retain all current apartheid legislation and restore separate development where it has been partially eroded. It advocates partition: each nation (race) would have its own area of jurisdiction. Indians would have part of Natal, Coloureds an area in the Western Cape, and the various black nations their present territories. The states would be politically independent but economically interdependent.

The CP advocates a relatively free economy, but in white South Africa white workers would be protected and there would be anti-monopoly legislation.

Herstigte Nasionale Party (HNP—Reformed National Party). The HNP, led by Mr. Jaap Marais, was formed in 1969 and won its first seat in Parliament in 1985. Its policy is very similar to that of the CP, and the two parties have jointly campaigned for seats in by-elections. Some members favor a merger of the two parties.

The HNP maintains that the task of the authorities should be to ensure full freedom for every citizen (*burgervryheid*), including religious freedom and freedom of speech, and to ensure that no group or organization obtains coercive power in society.

Like the CP, it advocates separate development with no integration between groups of different race, culture, language, or religion. It favors redistributing wealth to farmers and white couples with four or more children.

Inkatha Yenkululeko Yesizwe (Inkatha) (Organization for Freedom of the People). Inkatha, under the leadership of Zulu Chief Mangosuthu Gatsha Buthelezi, has approximately one million members, nearly all of whom are black. While about 85 percent are Zulus, the non-Zulu membership is growing: there are many Sothos in the Inkatha hierarchy, and the leader of the Youth Brigade, which has more than 480,000 members, is Sotho. The organization has over 2,000 branches, and the Tenth General Conference in 1984 was attended by 8,000 members and observers.

Inkatha's political position is moderate and similar to that of the Progressive Federal Party. In the past, both organizations have called for a national convention of representatives from all political

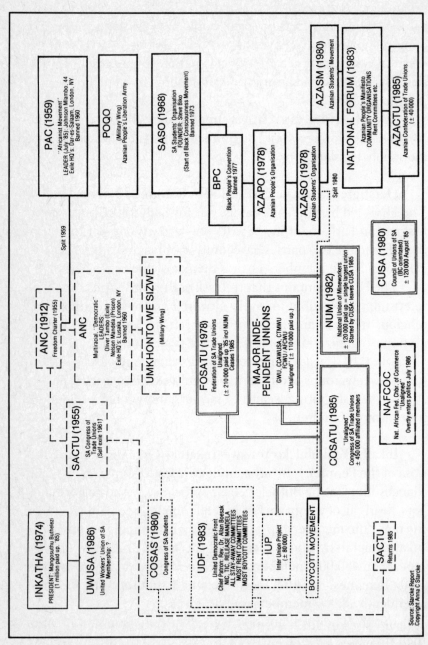

INKATHA (1974)
PRESIDENT: Mangosuthu Buthelezi
(1 million paid up. 85)

UWUSA (1986)
United Workers' Union of SA
Membership: ?

ANC (1912)
Freedom Charter (1955)

ANC
Multiracial. "Democratic"
LEADERS:
Oliver Tambo (Exile)
Nelson Mandela (Prison)
Exile HQ's Lusaka, London, NY
Banned 1960

SACTU (1955)
SA Congress of
Trade Unions
(Self exile 1961)

UMKHONTO WE SIZWE
(Military Wing)

PAC (1959)
"Africanist Movement"
LEADER (July 85): Johnson Mlambo. 44
Exile HQ's: Dar-es-Salaam, London. NY
Banned 1960

Split 1959

POQO
(Military Wing)
Azanian People's Liberation Army

SASO (1968)
SA Students' Organisation
FOUNDER: Steve Biko
(Start of Black Consciousness Movement)
Banned 1973

BPC
Black People's Convention
Banned 1977

AZAPO (1978)
Azanian People's Organisation

AZASO (1978)
Azanian Students' Organisation

Split 1980

AZASM (1980)
Azanian Students' Movement

NATIONAL FORUM (1983)
Azanian People's Manifesto
COMMUNITY ORGANISATIONS
Rent Committees etc.

AZACTU (1985)
Azanian Confederation of Trade Unions
(± 40 000)

CUSA (1980)
Council of Unions of SA
(BC orientated)
± 120 000 August 85

FOSATU (1978)
Federation of SA Trade Unions
Unaligned
(± 210 000 paid up '85 incl NUM)
Ceases 1985

**MAJOR INDE-
PENDENT UNIONS**
GWU, CCAWUSA, CTMWU
FOWU / AFCWU
"Unaligned" (± 110 000 paid up.)

NUM (1982)
National Union of Mineworkers
± 120 000 paid up = single largest union
Started by CUSA. leaves CUSA 1985

COSATU (1985)
"Unaligned"
Congress of SA Trade Unions
± 450 000 affiliated members

NAFCOC
Nat. African Fed. Chbr. of Commerce
"Unaligned"
Overtly enters politics July 1986

COSAS (1980)
Congress of SA Students

UDF (1983)
United Democratic Front
Chief Patron: Rev. Dr. Allan Boesak
NIC, TIC, RELEASE MANDELA
ALL STAY-AWAY COMMITTEES
MOST RENT COMMITTEES
MOST BOYCOTT COMMITTEES

IUP
Inter Union Project
(± 80 000)

BOYCOTT MOVEMENT

SACTU
Returns 1985

Source: Starcke Report
Copyright Anna C Starcke

Chart 3   Black Political and Labor Organizations

and pressure groups to map out South Africa's political future.

Inkatha is committed to achieving change, including the total eradication of apartheid, through nonviolent means. Chief Buthelezi is firmly committed to free enterprise as the economic system that will best serve the interests of the masses. He has said that the future holds the prospect of either a unitary state with universal suffrage as "the end product of an armed revolt," or a federal system of government as the "end product of the politics of negotiation." Although he supports the basic aims of the ANC's Freedom Charter, he has denounced the ANC's commitment to violence on the ground that it retards the process of black liberation.

Inkatha has never made a serious effort to recruit members outside the Zulu constituencies. This is perhaps unfortunate, as there may well be many moderate blacks who would feel comfortable with the Inkatha philosophy but who do not wish to belong to a group that is overwhelmingly Zulu.

Labour Party (LP).   The first general election to the "House of Representatives"—the Coloured chamber of the new tricameral parliament—was held on August 22, 1984. The Labour Party, led by Rev. Allan Hendrickse, won seventy-six of the eighty elected seats. As a consequence, it was accused by various black, Indian, and Coloured groups of "selling out" and was suspended from the South Africa Black Alliance.

The Labour Party agreed to participate in the new system on the ground that it was a step toward the dismantling of apartheid. The LP is committed to eradicating apartheid, opposes communism vigorously, and subscribes to democracy and the rule of law. It favors a mixed economy as a "happy medium" between capitalism and socialism.

The LP has a nonracial constitution. In addition to its Coloured members, it has about 200 black members, up to 1,000 white members, and a few hundred Indian members.

At the LP's annual congress in Kimberley in December 1984, Mr. Hendrickse proposed a federal system in which "racist" and "nonracist" states could coexist. A special committee was set up to research the question of a federal structure based on "one person, one vote" in a nonracial state.

National Forum (NF).   The National Forum is a loose grouping of black nationalist individuals and 200 organizations launched at Hammanskraal in June 1983 by AZAPO and various black consciousness luminaries. Saths Cooper, convener of the National Forum and the former leader of AZAPO, declines to estimate how many people support the organization, but it is apparently not yet strong enough to form a national movement.

The NF was set up primarily as a think tank to discuss and formulate policy for member organizations. Its position is unequivocally socialist. It envisages a future for Azania (South Africa) in which the black working classes will be acknowledged as the true leaders. Whites who want to contribute to the struggle should do so in their own constituencies.

The NF sees apartheid as a sociopolitical expression of "racial capitalism," or, in other words, as a system whereby the white state maintains economic hegemony by means of racial oppression.

The concept of "racial capitalism," now called "racialism and capitalism," was introduced to the black consciousness movement by Dr. Neville Alexander, who spent ten years on Robben Island followed by a five-year banning that expired in 1979. He reappeared to lend impetus and coherence to the Marxist element of the black consciousness movement.

The NF disagrees with the UDF's acceptance of the concept of different national groups, which coincides with the government position. It rejects the Freedom Charter and the Charter's recognition of the rights of different "national groups and races" to "use their own languages and develop their own folk culture and customs." It views the UDF and the ANC as anti-apartheid and reformist, but not revolutionary. It believes that the government recognizes this and, as a result, may legitimate the ANC.

The NF would have an Azania peopled only by Azanians, all speaking English and all paying allegiance to the nation rather than to any minority interests. Its manifesto pledges the movement "to struggle tirelessly for . . . the development of one national culture inspired by socialist values." Several of its constituent organizations are more interested in promoting a black Azania than a workers' Azania.

Natal Indian Congress (NIC).   The Natal Indian Congress is affiliated to the UDF and subscribes to the Freedom Charter. It strongly opposes the new constitution, which it sees as a means of entrenching racial oppression in South Africa.

It campaigned vociferously for a boycott of the 1984 elections and clashed publicly with the security police. Several of its leaders have been charged with high treason, and others have been detained without trial.

National Party (NP).   The National Party was formed in 1915 and has been the ruling party in South Africa since 1948.

In 1959 Dr. Verwoerd, then leader of the National Party, formulated a master plan for separate development in South Africa, based on the idea that different racial groups should live in homelands or national states having political autonomy. This plan was put into action and homeland states were formed. These were intended to satisfy black political aspirations. Because the NP did not consider it possible to identify and establish separate states for Indians and Coloureds, these groups had no representation in central government until the new constitution of 1983 was approved.*

The government has emphasized that the new constitution is a step in the process of constitutional development and that President P. W. Botha is committed to constitutional, social, and economic reform that will involve blacks in political decision making. There are major differences of opinion among party members as to what is meant by reform and change. President Botha is not prepared to

---

*Until September 3, 1984, only white South Africans were represented in Parliament. Then a new constitution came into effect, creating two additional houses: the House of Representatives for Coloureds, and the House of Delegates for Indians. Whites continue to be represented in the House of Assembly. This new system, with its tricameral parliament, represented many different things to South Africans and met with a wide variety of reactions. White nationalist groups saw it as a step in the direction of racial integration, which they rejected. There was a negative reaction on the part of many blacks, Indians, Coloureds, and whites, who saw it as a further entrenchment of racial separation and a reiteration of the refusal to grant blacks any kind of real political power. There was a positive response among many whites, Coloureds, and Indians who saw in it the thin edge of the wedge, a first move towards multiracial or nonracial society, which they welcomed. And there was a positive reaction among some who saw it as a solution to South Africa's problems.

offer any kind of blueprint for the future. But for the first time, groups outside the ruling party are able to make significant contributions toward policy formation through formal and informal channels.

National People's Party (NPP).   The National People's Party, led by Mr. Amichand Rajbansi, is an Indian party that won eighteen of the forty elected seats in the House of Delegates. It stands for the elimination through nonviolent means of racial, cultural, and sexual discrimination. Its following is estimated at around 29 percent of Indians.

New Republic Party (NRP).   The NRP was formed in 1977 and is generally regarded as the successor to the previous official opposition, the United Party. It has been weakened over the past few years by internal friction, financial problems, the loss of several by-elections, and the defection of three Members of Parliament to the NP. The party now has only five MPs, but remains strong in local government in Natal. Led by Mr. Bill Sutton, the party has a white membership but is prepared to accept Indians and Coloureds.

The NRP advocates a federal-confederal plan for South Africa in which there would be a "Common Area" occupied by whites, Coloureds, Indians, and urban blacks. Each racial group would have its own local authorities running community affairs. A federal council would provide cooperation between the groups in the common area. "Open areas" would be provided for those who did not wish to identify with any specific group. The common area and the independent homelands would form a confederation. A confederal assembly would administer matters of common concern delegated to it by agreement of the confederal states.

Pan-Africanist Congress (PAC).   The Pan-Africanist Congress, formed in 1959, has been prevented by serious internal conflicts from being effective inside or outside South Africa. The PAC's central committee suffered a three-way split in 1984, and the Congress has been plagued by questions about its role, given the strong support among blacks for the ANC, whose platform is very similar to its own.

Progressive Federal Party (PFP). The Progressive Federal Party was formed in 1977 and is the official opposition to the ruling National Party. The PFP was originally a white party, but when legislation prohibiting multiracial parties was repealed it opened its membership and is now actively recruiting all races.

The PFP supports equal citizenship rights for all South Africans; shared political rights; religious freedom and the right of people to maintain their own language and culture; equality of opportunity; and the protection of property rights. It advocates a fairly free economy combined, at least initially, with considerable state welfare, and it opposes group domination and statutory apartheid. It has called for the release of Nelson Mandela and other political detainees, the unbanning of political organizations, and an end to the state of emergency.

The PFP has been the most vociferous of the groups calling for a national convention at which representatives of all South Africa's major groups would draw up a new constitution. Inkatha and the Labour Party have also expressed support for a national convention, while the NP, CP, and AZAPO are against it.

SABRA. SABRA is a white nationalist organization formed in 1948. Its 4,000 paid-up members do not see themselves as a political group but as an Afrikaner scientific/educational society organized to provide scientific information regarding relations between races and nations.

SABRA advocates the development of free, democratic nation-states with free enterprise economies, which would cooperate on matters of common interest. These states would be based on racial segregation and the primary aim would be to secure the future of whites.

Sofasonke Party. The Sofasonke Party is a moderate black party that operates primarily in the Vaal Triangle. It claims a registered membership of 180,000 spread among thirty-three branches. The party has a majority in the Soweto City Council and plans to establish itself nationally. It concerns itself mainly with local politics, and its membership is open to Coloureds. It believes that peaceful, constructive participation is the route to reform. There are similar parties in other urban areas.

Solidarity.   Solidarity is an Indian party formed in January 1984 to participate in the election to the House of Delegates. Led by Mr. J. N. Reddy, Solidarity won seventeen of the forty elected seats. It favors free enterprise, a unitary education system, and a bill of rights guaranteeing individual freedoms. Like the NPP, its main objective is to promote a nonracial society through consultation rather than confrontation. It does not see any marked differences between its policies and those of the NPP.

United Democratic Front (UDF).   The United Democratic Front was launched by Rev. Allan Boesak and others in Cape Town in 1983. It claims the support of two million people belonging to its 648 affiliate organizations, which range from small, insignificant groups to important and influential organizations. (The figure of two million is reached by counting all the members of all the affiliates and does not take into account overlapping memberships.) Most of the groups under the UDF umbrella, such as the Transvaal Indian Congress, are racially defined, and include trade unions and civic associations.

The UDF's sole formal manifesto is the Declaration of the United Democratic Front, which calls for "a united, democratic South Africa based on the will of the people." It gives no details that expand on this. Many UDF affiliates support the Freedom Charter, which they regard as the embodiment of the liberation movement. The UDF opposes the use of violence.

The UDF is regarded by many as the legitimate front of the ANC. This may or may not be true. But both subscribe to the Freedom Charter, and Zinzi Mandela, daughter of the ANC's Nelson Mandela, has given the UDF her public blessing.

Some UDF affiliates have joined the call for a national convention, while others, among them Mr. Cassim Saloojee, UDF treasurer, have argued that a national convention cannot be held "when our true leaders are still in detention, banned, or in exile."

There is no love lost between the National Forum and the UDF. Ideological differences have recently resulted in open warfare, especially among students, and campuses and hostels have become the settings for knife battles, stabbings, and persecutions.

Trade Unions

Trade unions in South Africa are highly politicized. Various unions reflect the political positions of all the major parties and pressure groups we have discussed.

Congress of South African Trade Unions (COSATU). COSATU is the most recent federation of trade unions to appear on the South African scene, and possibly the biggest. Launched in November 1985, it has thirty-three affiliates representing "nearly 450,000 workers." It is nonracial but predominantly black. It is not aligned to any political party but has a position similar to that of the UDF.

Council of Unions of South Africa (CUSA). CUSA has twelve affiliates and approximately 120,000 paid-up members. It is open to workers of all races but reserves leadership posts for blacks. Its position is similar to that of the National Forum.

South African Confederation of Labour (SACLA). SACLA has twelve affiliates and about 124,400 members. Its membership is exclusively white and about 40 percent are state employees. The two main affiliates are the Mine Workers' Union and the South African Iron, Steel and Allied Industries Union, both of which favor apartheid.

The Emerging and Established Union Movements. COSATU and CUSA, along with about thirty-five unaffiliated unions — notably the African Food and Canning Workers' Union; the Commercial, Catering and Allied Workers' Union of South Africa; the General Workers' Union; the National Union of Mineworkers; and the South African Allied Workers' Union — are sometimes collectively known as the emerging union movement, which is racially mixed but predominantly black. They have been responsible for increased strike action, boycotts, and stay-aways. Some unionists see them as the only legal outlets for black political aspirations.

The established union movement consists of SACLA and more than 100 unaffiliated registered unions. The number of whites-only registered unions has dropped dramatically—from seventy-one in 1982 to forty-three in 1983.

The total membership of all unions in South Africa is about 12.4 percent of the economically active population (including the ten homelands). This is far lower than the percentages in most European democracies, where 50 to 80 percent of the work force is unionized. It is closer to unionization rates in the United States and the capitalist countries of the Pacific.

Homeland Political Parties

In the homelands there are many black political parties, some with large followings. They are ethnically homogeneous and all oppose laws that discriminate on racial grounds. Most, but not all, favor some kind of homeland policy and, ultimately, a Southern African federation or confederation. Homeland parties generally rely on tribal loyalties, and traditional chiefs are prominent in most of them.

The Natal-KwaZulu Indaba

In Natal, representatives from a wide variety of interest groups formed the Natal-KwaZulu Indaba in 1986 in an attempt to agree on economic and constitutional proposals for a post-apartheid Natal. Delegates of all races from the farming community, business, industry, women's groups, and mainstream political groups met for two days every week to consider various proposals. The Indaba agreed on a very general Bill of Rights and drew up a constitutional proposal for a bicameral legislature in Natal, with one house based on ethnicity and the other on universal suffrage.

Other Pressure Groups

The nature of the problems confronting South Africa has fostered a high degree of political consciousness. As a result, organizations formed for entirely different reasons have become political pressure groups. There are many examples — too many to mention — but they fall into the following main categories.

Black, white, and mixed students' organizations represent all the main positions from white to black nationalism, Marxism to free enterprise, and violent confrontation to peaceful dialogue.

The Civic Associations movement, started by the Committee of Ten in Soweto in the 1970s under the chairmanship of Dr. Ntatho Motlana, concerns itself primarily with local government issues in black and Coloured townships. Unlike Sofasonke, it is firmly opposed to participation in urban council elections.

The churches are involved in the debate to varying degrees. The South African Council of Churches rose to prominence under Bishop Desmond Tutu's leadership in the 1970s. It supports the UDF and is the South African counterpart of the World Council of Churches. The two major Afrikaner churches, the Nederduits Gereformeerde Kerk (NGK) and the Nederduits Hervormde Kerk van Afrika (NHK), in the past have contributed to the conviction among Afrikaners that apartheid is consistent with the scriptures. The NGK has now renounced racism, and this should have a significant impact on Afrikaner thinking.

Organized business groups are playing an increasingly overt political role, as are institutes, welfare and service groups, and public policy and cultural groups. In addition, there are numerous international anti-apartheid and "Friends of South Africa" organizations.

Conclusion

Almost all these political groups are characterized primarily by opposition politics. It is clear what they are against; it is not at all clear what they are for. None of them, except for the classical Marxists and the Afrikaner nationalists, have offered concrete proposals for the future.

Moreover, no single group is representative of anything approaching a majority of the population. The UDF and Inkatha claim memberships of around two million and one million respectively, but even these numbers are small in relation to a South African adult population of approximately fifteen million. So we have many small divergent groups, few of which have any clear direction, policy, or constituency.

The extreme black nationalists (AZAPO and the National Forum) and the extreme white nationalists (the AWB, HNP, and CP) reject each other, yet share a lot of common ground in terms of racial exclusion. Both aim to take control of the country and impose their systems on everyone else.

The more moderate groupings—the ANC, UDF, NP, NRP, PFP, Inkatha, and so on—talk about equal rights, recognition for national groups, devolution, and power-sharing, but none of them articulate clearly what these concepts imply.

What is clear is that most white South Africans and many Indians and Coloureds will strongly resist the formation of a unitary state with a centrally controlled economy and massive wealth redistribution. Afrikaner nationalists in particular would fight to the bitter end against any system that would rob them of their cultural identity. At the same time, blacks, Coloureds, and Indians will not settle for anything less than full South African citizenship and political equality with white South Africans.

In a television news program South African businessmen who met with ANC representatives in Lusaka reported that they had been unable to agree with the ANC "on economic policy." The question one must ask is, why were they trying to agree? Why were they not considering an option in which each group could pursue its own economic policy? The answer is that they were locked into a debate based on the collectivist assumptions that the "winner takes all" and "unity is strength."

As long as these remain the underlying assumptions, South African political life will be marked by escalating conflict and bloodshed. The current impasse in South Africa exists because all the various options under debate lead to a dead end. If you were to ask supporters of any of the political parties or alliances whether they think their organization could bring peace and prosperity to the country, most would say no. Very few people think that their own group really has a solution; most expect continued and escalating conflict, and desire only that their group should preside over it.

But there is another option, and that is to replace confrontational politics with a "multi-option" system in which strength lies in diversity. There is only one way in which the wide diversity of social, cultural, ethnic, and political aspirations of South Africans can be accommodated: the country must be divided into states or cantons, each governing itself according to the dictates of its citizens. Central government must be constitutionally limited to a few general areas of jurisdiction that are agreed upon by all the cantons and that do not provoke conflict.

In such a system, every person born in greater South Africa, regardless of race or nationality, would be a South African citizen with the same rights as every other citizen. Each adult would have the vote and all political parties would be free to participate in elections in any or all of the autonomous districts. All major groups would govern sizable areas and run them in their own way. Freedom of movement would be entrenched in the constitution, so that if an HNP supporter found himself in an AZAPO area, he would be free to move to an HNP or CP canton, and vice versa.

The only political group that stands to lose power under this system is the NP. But the NP has already accepted the principles of power-sharing and devolution, and in a canton system it would continue to control certain areas for many years. The alternatives it now faces are less appealing: it might find itself out of government altogether, or it may soon be presiding over a bloodbath.

PART THREE

The Solution

Part Three provides a blueprint for a canton system in
South Africa and explains how this would accommodate
all the current political parties and pressure groups. The
optimal judicial system for such a form of government
is discussed, as well as various economic policy options
that cantons might pursue. The section ends with a
detailed strategy for popularizing and implementing the
proposed system.

CHAPTER 10

Cantons: A Political Solution

The essential feature of the Swiss Commonwealth is that it is a genuine and natural democracy.

—Albert Venn Dicey

The Swiss Model

IN OUR SEARCH for a political system that meets all the disparate and conflicting requirements of South Africa's heterogeneous peoples, we can learn much from Switzerland. The Swiss system is so extraordinarily appropriate for South Africa—even more so than for Switzerland itself—that we could take their constitution, almost verbatim, and transplant it to South Africa.

Switzerland is a tiny, mountainous, and landlocked territory with no mineral wealth and poor agricultural potential. Forests, hills, mountains, and rocky terrain constitute two-thirds of the total land area. The population is heterogeneous. While approximately two-thirds of the population speak German, no single ethnolinguistic group has a majority in all cantons or communes.

Despite these potential constraints, Switzerland has not only survived—it has prospered. It is an extremely rich country with one of the highest living standards in Europe, high growth rates, low inflation, low unemployment, and low social conflict. When wars have raged around it, Switzerland has remained at peace. What has made this miracle possible?

The answer lies in the country's political system and the economic and social consequences of that system. This is the key to Switzerland's success, and it is from this that we can learn in South Africa.

Why Is Switzerland Relevant?

South Africa is a unique country with unique problems. Clearly it will have to develop its own solutions based on the needs of its own people. But we do not need to re-invent the wheel. All we need do is modify it to suit our needs. Fortuitously, Switzerland provides us with a remarkably apt working model in which many of the problems that face South Africa today have been confronted and solved through trial and error over several centuries.

The Swiss system originated in the thirteenth century among people very primitive by twentieth century standards. In the course of 700 years, during which there were numerous civil wars, a true democracy was established. Today, people with disparate needs and interests live, each according to their own values, in peace and prosperity. This extraordinary testimony to the degree of devolution and democracy attainable in a diverse society demonstrates that South Africa's diversity can become its strength.

The Swiss System

Switzerland, with an area of 41,293 square kilometers, is slightly smaller than Transkei (43,000 square kilometers). It is densely populated, with around six and a half million people, which means, if we include uninhabited areas, a density of 250 people per square kilometer.

There are four national languages in Switzerland: German, French, Italian, and Rhaeto-Romansch. Sixty-five percent of the population is German-speaking, eighteen percent French, ten percent Italian, and one percent Rhaeto-Romansch. Six percent, mostly migrant workers, speak other languages. Within the four main language groups there are many local dialects.

The Cantons.   In 1291, the first mutual assistance pact between three independent cantons was agreed to. The alliance was based on the principle of equality, a principle that remains the basis of the canton system today. Thus Swiss history has led, not to a centralized state, but to a "nation by will." Small communities of varying size, economic strength, and cultural tradition live voluntarily and in mutual respect in the same federal state.

The federal state comprises twenty-six autonomous cantons and half-cantons. They vary in size from Basle City, with an area of 37.2 square kilometers, to Bern, which covers 6,049.4 square kilometers, and in population from as few as 12,800 people in Appenzell to 1,124,200 people in Zurich. Six of the cantons have fewer than 50,000 people, four have between 50,000 and 100,000, ten between 100,000 and 300,000, and five have between 300,000 and 900,000. Each canton has its own constitution and laws. The cantonal legislative authority is a one-chamber parliament that in most cantons is elected by proportional representation. The smallest cantonal council has fifty-one members; the largest, two hundred. Each canton parliament has an executive body of five to eight members elected by the citizens of the canton. Nineteen cantons have a majority of German-speakers, six a majority of French speakers, and one a majority of Italian speakers.

Five small cantons in eastern and central Switzerland have a truly democratic tradition of "Landsgemeinde," or "open-air" parliaments. Once a year the electorate assembles in the open air to elect the cantonal government and select members of the Councils of State by a show of hands. They settle many other important matters by public debate and a show of hands.

Each canton organizes its administration in its own way, but the usual divisions are Interior, Justice and Police, Military, Finance, Economy, Health, Social Care, Education, and Public Buildings and Works. Cantons are responsible for their own judiciary and have their own courts, police, jails, and reformatories. They finance their activities primarily through income and property taxes levied on their own citizens and residents. Because they vary so much in size, economic strength, and population, their budgets range from a few million to thousands of millions of francs.

Communes.   Within the cantons there are about 3,000 communities or communes with rights and duties laid down by the cantons. Some regions have a long tradition of communal autonomy, whereas others have always been more centralized. One indication of the degree of autonomy enjoyed by the communes is that they levy their own taxes on their residents.

Like the cantons, communes vary greatly in size, from tiny communities in the mountains with only a few dozen inhabitants to great cities like Zurich, Bern, and Geneva. Some of the large communities are bigger than the smallest cantons.

Each commune has a constitution setting out the powers granted it by its canton. People's rights to referendums and "initiatives" are generally well developed and widely recognized.

In many small communes every adult citizen with the right to vote can participate in the communal assembly. Large communes have a parliament and usually administer canton and federal legislation in addition to their own policies.

Examples of areas in which communes typically have autonomy are: schools, energy, refuse collection, building regulations, traffic regulations, public parks, bridges, roads, police, fire services, health departments, social care, and sports. Communes often form regional associations to deal with matters such as refuse collection, sewage disposal, and public works.

The Federal Assembly (Parliament)

Between the beginning of the Swiss confederation, in 1291, and 1948, many more cantons joined the original three, but their only important common bond was a willingness to hand over the right of making peace and war to the central government. They shared little else, not even the same systems of measurement or a common currency. In 1847, civil war between the cantons frightened them into tightening their links and, in 1848, a new constitution was adopted.

This constitution allowed each canton to retain sovereignty over its domestic affairs, but a few tasks thought to be of common concern were assigned to the Confederation (central government). Article 2 of the Federal Constitution lists three purposes of the Confederation: "To assert the independence of the Fatherland from the outside world; maintenance of the law and order within; protection of the freedom and rights of the citizens of the Confederation and promotion of their common welfare." The original intention was to restrict federal responsibility to foreign policy, national defense, arbitration of inter-cantonal disputes, and the guarantee of individual rights and freedom of trade and commerce. These areas have grown during the past 130 years to include customs, the mint, the post office, telecommunications, and the federal railway.

The Swiss Federal Assembly consists of two houses:

The National Council.   This is the direct representative of the people. Its 200 seats are distributed among the various cantons on the basis of population, but each canton or half-canton, even the smallest, has at least one representative. In general elections, each canton constitutes a constituency. The President of the National Council is elected for one year. In terms of protocol, this is the highest official post in the Confederation.

The Council of States.   Here the cantons are represented equally, regardless of size. Each canton sends two members and half-cantons send one. The cantons decide independently how to elect members and how long they should hold office. Most elect members by ballot for four years.

The National Council and the Council of States hold four regular sessions per year, each lasting three weeks. They have equal status, and every parliamentary bill has to be debated and approved in each house. If there are differences of opinion between the Councils, they pass the issue back and forth. Because the forty-six members of the Council of States have the same power as the 200 members of the National Council, minority groups in small cantons are protected from being overruled by big cantons.

The two houses meet to form the Joint Federal Assembly only

in order to pass federal laws, ratify state treaties, and elect Federal Councillors and judges. The legislative decisions of Parliament are not final, however, because they are subject to the Referendum.

There are two types of referendum in Switzerland: the Obligatory Referendum, which is used at federal or cantonal level to ensure that all constitutional changes are put to the popular vote, and the Optional Referendum, which enables the public to have its say about any federal policy, legislation, or general decree. An optional referendum is held if a minimum of 50,000 citizens or eight cantons request it within ninety days of the official publication of a new measure.

The Federal Council

The Federal Executive (cabinet) is composed of seven equally ranked ministers who are elected individually for four-year terms by the Joint Federal Assembly. Each minister is responsible for a department that he or she represents within the Federal Council. Every year, one of the Federal Councillors is elected by the Federal Assembly to the post of Federal President. The only extra responsibilities this position entails are to chair meetings of the Federal Council and to undertake a few protocol duties. Thus the President is essentially no more than the cabinet chairman for one year.

All four main political parties are represented at cabinet level. Theoretically, any Swiss citizen may become a Councillor, but no canton may have more than one representative in the cabinet at the same time, and traditionally at least two of the seven belong to a linguistic minority.

General Comments

Over the past seven centuries, Switzerland has developed a political system that recognizes the needs of heterogeneous population groups with different languages, cultures, traditions, and temperaments.

It is a system that may be summarized as "one person, many votes." Swiss citizens vote for representatives at community, canton, and federal levels. They petition for referendums on specific measures at all three levels. In addition, the Constitution allows for popular initiatives. If the signatures of at least 100,000 voters are obtained, an initiative can propose an addition to or a deletion from the Federal Constitution. The initiative is discussed by both houses and then put to popular vote.

In recent years, for instance, there have been initiatives in favor of extra air pollution devices in motor vehicles, lawful abortion, the introduction of VAT (value added tax), and grants for universities and research. All of these were rejected. New constitutional articles on equal rights for men and women and consumer protection were accepted.

Every Swiss citizen can thus play an effective part in the decision making process. New laws are not easily introduced. Indeed, the Swiss boast that "we never accept anything unless it has been presented to us at least twice," and it is joked that when the Swiss vote on measures proposed by their politicians, they usually vote no.

The Swiss system ensures that there is neither majority nor minority group domination, and that one political party cannot impose its will on the whole country. In this sense, Switzerland probably represents the democratic ideal more closely than any other country.

The Swiss system is open and flexible, permitting changes and developments in response to diverse popular wishes. Some cantons have divided into half-cantons, each fully autonomous, while others have merged. Boundaries have shifted and changed. Cantons and communes have formed and dissolved alliances and joint ventures. The laws and policies reflect geographic and community differences (see Appendix III).

Because the powers of the Federal Assembly are severely restricted and the Councillors' functions are purely administrative, few people in Switzerland even know who the Federal President is in any given year. There is no incentive for hard-fought winner-take-all political campaigns at the national level because the major political issues are essentially localized. National political life is completely devolved and fragmented. Great political demonstrations, passionate debates, and spectacular confrontations are rare. Because government has few conflict-provoking powers and functions, Swiss society is blissfully depoliticized.

Freedom of movement of goods, capital, and people between cantons is entrenched in the Constitution. Consequently, even those cantons in which socialist parties predominate have relatively free economic policies, because if they increase taxes and controls unduly, their residents simply vote with their feet and move to another canton. Conversely, free market parties maintain basic welfare programs. In general, there is a tendency towards minimal government with concomitantly high levels of personal freedom.

Because most government functions are located at the local level, there is a permanent demonstration effect. In other words, there is a continuing visible test of alternative policies within one country, so that society tends towards the optimal policy on any given issue, and there is a spontaneous discipline away from unsuccessful or unproductive policies. Political competition tends to produce benefits in much the same way that economic competition does.

CHAPTER 11

A Canton System
for South Africa

*All history teaches that in small states there tends, other
things being equal, to be more personal freedom, more
individuality and a higher social vitality than in large. I
believe a body of small, highly organized social units
self-governing, but uniting together for the furtherance of
certain great common aims, to be the highest form of social
organization yet evolved by humanity.*
— Olive Schreiner, 1908

ANY FUTURE POLITICAL DISPENSATION for South Africa clearly
must be based on a system that ensures that all its disparate groups
can live without fear of domination by any other group. The Swiss
system offers many socioeconomic options for catering to the
conflicting needs of Switzerland's four main national groups and
various subgroups. In South Africa, there are more social, cultural,
and ethnic groupings than in Switzerland. We thus have an even
greater need for a diversity of political options.

It is for this reason that we propose a canton system for South
Africa as the only structure through which our country can achieve
enduring peace and prosperity for all its people. We recommend a

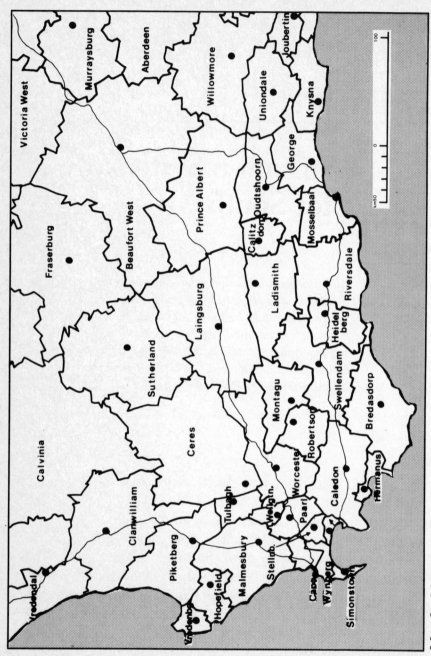

Map 3　Magisterial Districts—Cape Province

system that splits the country into numerous autonomous cantons, linked by a central government whose functions are strictly limited by a constitution that entrenches equality before the law for every individual and does not entail the subjugation of minorities or individuals.

Structure and Powers of Cantons

Political Diversity.   Each canton would have its own parliament, and possibly its own constitution, as determined by referendum. Constitutions would probably vary a great deal from one district to another. Different political groupings would form in different areas with varying proposals. For example, the ANC might propose a form of socialism based on the Freedom Charter in areas where it enjoys majority support. The PFP would probably suggest some kind of social democracy in, for example, Northern Johannesburg, where it has strong support. A kaleidoscope of opinions and ideologies could and would be accommodated.

There would be universal suffrage for the de facto residents of each canton until a canton parliament is elected. Thereafter, each canton would decide, within constitutional limits, how much say its residents would have on future issues and what method of voting would be adopted. A canton might choose proportional representation, a Westminster-type system, or a one-party state. Each canton would send representatives to the central government. These would be chosen by plebiscite or canton government decree, again depending on each canton's policy.

The focus of political party action would be at canton level. Some political parties might encompass several or many cantons, while others might operate only in one canton. One would expect all the current political pressure groups to be active, and probably others too.

Administrative Diversity.   The functions of central government would be drastically limited, as the cantons would control all but a few aspects of administration. Should they so wish, the cantons could devolve power further to local authorities equivalent to the Swiss communities. Each canton would determine its own degree of devolution. Some, no doubt, would be run entirely by a central body, while others would decentralize almost all aspects of administration to local authorities, as proposed by Denis Beckett in *Permanent Peace*. In the case of local authorities representing large areas or cities, there could be further devolution to groups similar to existing taxpayer associations. These would control all matters of local concern such as shopping hours, street lights, racial policy, zoning and building regulations, and so on.

Cantons or local authorities would be free to organize themselves into alliances or groupings for administrative purposes. They might wish to share, for example, the administration of policing, transport, water supplies, power, sewage disposal, or rubbish collection. Alternatively, they might contract out any or all of these services to private companies, which could supply the needs of one or many cantons.

Economic Diversity.   Each canton would determine its own economic policy, its own labor, transport, education, tax, subsidization, welfare, and race policies.

Central government would have no authority to grant monopolies to, for example, the Putco Bus Company, or legislate against "pirate" taxis. Each canton would decide for itself whether to have an open market in transportation, to license taxis restrictively, to have transport subsidies, or to provide canton public transport.

It is both foolish and unfair to have one set of electrification standards or slaughterhouse standards — or any other standards — for the whole country. Such regulations do not result in the stated intention of high standards for all. Instead, they price homes, transport, clothing, food, and whatever else is regulated out of reach of the poor. As we discussed in Chapter 4, standards regulations usually amount to disguised discrimination against lower socioeconomic groups. They protect only vested interests parading themselves as advocates of the "public interest." One consequence of devolution would be a built-in protection of the public from such abuse of government power.

Racial Policy. Racial policy is discussed at the end of Chapter 13 under the subheading "Racial Discrimination."

Citizenship. Canton governments would have the right to grant or refuse citizenship in their cantons to newcomers. There are good reasons for permitting this. Although freedom of movement in and out of cantons would be constitutionally entrenched, cantons should be able to restrict citizenship to discourage excessive immigration, to maintain their political character, or to raise revenue by selling citizenship, as in Switzerland. The more attractive a canton's policies, the more revenue it could raise in this way.

Advantages of Diversity

There are two very important advantages to a diversity of economic, political, and social policies. The first is that diversity is truly democratic. The greater the diversity, the more real choices people have, and the greater the likelihood that they will be able to live in a way that coincides with their own values.

Second, there is a permanent demonstration effect. People can see from day to day which tax policy, which housing policy, which race policy, which subsidy policy produces the best results.

The Demonstration Effect. The main reason why a system with severe restrictions on central government creates enduring peace and prosperity is that political competition occurs between the constituent states or cantons.

Two half-cantons in Switzerland, Basle City and Basle Country, provide a striking example of this. Basle Country decreased taxes and experienced high growth, while Basle City increased taxes and stagnated. Between 1970 and 1980, over 13 percent of Basle City's residents moved into the suburbs (Basle Country). Eventually Basle City was forced to reduce taxation to bring it more into line with Basle Country.

Thus the demonstration effect prevents Switzerland's socialist cantons from burdening their economies with excessive regulations and taxes; if they try to do so, they simply lose people and wealth

to neighboring cantons with more attractive policies. Canton governments also lose votes if they cannot maintain levels of growth
and welfare comparable to those in other cantons. The result is that
even those Swiss cantons with radical socialist governments have
some of the freest economies in Europe, while even the most laissez-
faire cantons maintain basic welfare programs.

The demonstration effect is apparent to a lesser extent throughout the world. There is a virtually direct correlation between free
market policies and prosperity. Countries with a high degree of government intervention typically exhibit low growth and underdevelop-
ment, instability, conflict, and oppression. A recent World Bank study
found that this correlation generally holds true regardless of the size
of a country, its ethnicity, its natural resource endowment, or its level
of development. High growth tends to bring with it high life expectancy, low infant mortality rates, low divorce rates, low social problems, reduced violence, and even less aggressiveness toward other
countries.

Freedom of Movement

Complete freedom of movement for people and wealth is the crucial ingredient in our canton formula. The demonstration effect can
work properly only if people are able to vote with their feet by moving from one canton to another, taking their wealth and productivity
with them.

If AZAPO-ruled cantons were to introduce full-blown Marxism with disastrous consequences, people would be able simply to
move to or seek jobs in cantons with greater wealth and freedom.
Conversely, if Marxism were to provide the level of welfare and
benefits it promises, Marxist cantons would attract more people, and
other cantons would follow their example.

Secession

Every canton should have the right to secede. This provides an
important safety valve for the system. Switzerland shows that socialist
and laissez-faire cantons can operate comfortably side by side in one

country. However, there is still the possibility that radical white or black nationalist cantons might find themselves unable to agree on the general principles that the great majority of cantons want entrenched in the constitution. Or they might find the central government's defense, foreign trade, or immigration policy unacceptable.

To save the country from being torn apart by civil war, these cantons should have the right to secede if a given percentage of the population in a canton, let us say 75 percent, vote to do so. For practical reasons this option would seldom, if ever, be exercised, but it should be available nonetheless. Perhaps a number of radical black nationalist cantons would want to form a breakaway alliance in an unlimited centralized state. If, in time, the differences that led to secession were overcome or came to be seen as less important, the breakaway cantons could be readmitted to the country.

The Swiss Constitution recognizes the right of secession, but it has never been exercised. On the contrary, other areas have wanted to join. A canton system with minimal centralization reduces conflict and division and leads to harmony and inclusion. There is a good chance that neighboring territories such as Lesotho and Swaziland would eventually apply for some kind of confederal relationship with South Africa. If they were not included from the start, the four independent homelands would probably seek inclusion, and possibly South West Africa/Namibia as well.

Expulsion

The other side of the right to secede is the possibility of expulsion. If a canton persists in some policy that all the others find unacceptable, there should be a procedure whereby it can be expelled. Expulsion, being a drastic measure, should require a unanimous or near-unanimous vote in favor by all the cantons other than the one under scrutiny. Alternatively, a referendum could be held in all cantons other than the one in question, with a specified majority necessary in order for expulsion to take place. In the unlikely event of an expulsion, all the citizens of the expelled canton should retain the right to hold South African citizenship and the right to move freely into an area remaining within South Africa.

Determination of Cantons

South Africa currently has 306 magisterial districts, some of which are divided into subdistricts (detached magistrates), with an average population of 80,000 per district. None is as small as the smallest Swiss cantons. These magisterial districts have existing judicial and administrative infrastructures and nonideological boundaries that form sensible administrative units. These boundaries are determined by recommendation of the Commission for Administration, an independent statutory body responsible for purely administrative and manpower matters. The functions that usually coincide with magisterial districts include:

- criminal and civil courts
- licensing offices
- receivers of revenue
- public works
- school boards
- labor bureaus
- welfare offices
- population registration
- police districts
- various inspectorates

Some magisterial district boundaries correspond to the distribution of socioeconomic populations. This is partly a consequence of past legislation separating races into different areas, but it would occur to some extent in any heterogeneous country, regardless of racial or political policy, simply because people generally choose to live among those with whom they identify.

Magisterial districts are the most logical and least contentious starting points for the creation of cantons. We propose, therefore, that South Africa be divided into cantons corresponding to existing magisterial districts. In many areas, of course, there may be valid geographic, social, linguistic, ethnic, cultural, or economic reasons for consolidating two or more districts, splitting districts, or moving boundaries. There are several feasible ways to finalize canton boundaries. We offer the following proposals in the belief that they will be found acceptable by most people.

Canton Judicial Delimitation Commission

In order to defuse and depoliticize the formation of cantons as much as possible, a Judicial Delimitation Commission should be established. It would consist of judges and magistrates, preferably drawn from all the main groupings, who are not identified with any political ideology. They should take an oath committing themselves to the lack of bias that their judicial office requires.

The Commission would receive evidence concerning canton boundaries. It should not be subject to political control, and its members should have absolute discretion to weigh objectively all the evidence presented to them and to act accordingly. There would be a rebuttable presumption in favor of existing magisterial districts. In other words, people would have to offer evidence as to why a magisterial district should not become a separate canton.

Anyone must be free to present submissions in favor of, or in opposition to, existing magisterial boundaries. For example, arguments could be based on geographic or ethnic features, on the principle of separating urban and rural areas, or simply on grounds of practical administration. Evidence could include anything from public opinion surveys to crime rates, from stages of development to climatic conditions.*

We recommend a *judicial* commission because we can think of no other politically acceptable way for the government of the day to win widespread support for these reforms. Although it will always

---

* Different groups would sometimes present conflicting evidence. The Johannesburg Central Business District Association might argue convincingly for a "metropolitan" canton including Soweto, Roodepoort, Dobsonville, Johannesburg, Diepmeadow, Edenvale, Sandton, and Randburg. Conversely, a strong case could be made, primarily on ethnic and socioeconomic grounds, for establishing greater Soweto (including Dobsonville and Diepmeadow) as an independent canton.

Purely administrative considerations might lead to calls for consolidating Johannesburg, Sandton, and Randburg. Or perhaps it would be argued that each of these fairly large municipalities should become a separate canton that would cooperate with the other two on issues such as water, electricity, and sewage reticulation.

It would probably not be advisable to split villages with a few thousand people of various racial groups into two or three cantons based on ethnicity. Geographic or administrative considerations would prevail here. However, this would not preclude a division along ethnic lines should the people concerned vote for it in a referendum initiated (by petition) to challenge a ruling of the Delimitation Commission.

have its critics, the South African judiciary is still regarded by most people of goodwill as reasonably independent. It is more likely to make good decisions, to be impartial, and to have legitimacy in the eyes of most South Africans than any other institution in or out of the country.

While we have said that all evidence, including that based on ethnicity, should be admissible, we recognize that the idea of political entities based on racial, cultural, or linguistic grounds is automatically linked with apartheid and the homelands in South Africa. As such, it tends to have negative connotations. This is unfortunate. In the course of this chapter, we have made clear that our proposal is based on the total dismantling of all vestiges of apartheid and the creation of a genuine democracy, with full equality before the law regardless of race and with more constitutionally entrenched rights and freedoms than exist in even the freest societies at present. In addition, it should be borne in mind that all over the world countries have been politically subdivided according to ethnic and cultural criteria. This is largely the basis on which Belgium and the Netherlands, for example, are politically organized.

Referendum — the Final Arbiter

If the citizens of two districts wish to merge, or if part of a district wishes to break off and become independent or be incorporated into another area, then referendums must be held in the areas concerned. Those from whom separation is sought, however, would not vote. Before a referendum concerning canton boundaries is held, a petition signed by 10 percent of the voters in the area that wishes to change should be required for presentation to the Delimitation Commission.

The freedom of minorities to break away and join other cantons or become independent would be a very important factor encouraging majority groups to consider the wishes of minorities they do not want to lose. It would thus discourage bad government; if majorities misbehave, minorities will leave or vote for separation.

The Delimitation Commission should be a permanent body, reconvened from time to time (as are constitutional conventions in

Switzerland) to consider further boundary changes. The formation of cantons should be a dynamic and continuing process of redefinition and re-examination according to the people's wishes.

Homelands and National States

In South Africa the homeland concept is extremely unpopular. This is because the homelands have developed hand in hand with apartheid, and with influx control in particular.

As we observed in Chapter 3, over three million people have been forcibly relocated from white to black areas as a consequence of this policy. Homes have been split apart as men and women have been forced to leave their families in the homelands to seek work in white cities or industrial "growth points." The movement of these migrant laborers has been subject to numerous controls, and people working or living illegally in white areas have been fined or imprisoned. (Most of these injustices ceased with the repeal of influx control laws in mid-1986.)

For many educated urban blacks the idea of ethnic identification is linked firmly to the homeland concept and is therefore unacceptable. They stress that it is important in their struggle for liberation for all black South Africans to identify themselves as one group. This is one reason why any constitutional proposal that includes provisions based on ethnicity is unlikely to succeed in our country.

However, in the absence of coercion or racially discriminatory legislation, there is no reason why the homelands should not be included as ethnic cantons if they so wish. They should have the freedom to decide, preferably by referendum, whether they wish to be independent states or autonomous cantons. All of their citizens should have the right to choose South African or homeland citizenship or both.

With South African citizenship they would be able to move freely between their homeland and South Africa, and remain permanently in the canton of their choice should they so wish. This would encourage homeland leaders to govern well, and would ensure that all people living in homelands would be doing so through choice.

Several of the homelands and national states form sensible units as they are. Transkei, for example, has fairly logical boundaries. In the case of Ciskei, however, evidence might be presented for the inclusion of the Border Region. The split between Natal and KwaZulu is arbitrary and people in these two regions would have to decide whether they wish to form one canton (the increasingly popular "Kwa-Natal" idea) or several. Certain parts of Bophutha-tswana such as Thaba N'chu could become independent cantons or merge with others. Those homelands that are not contiguous units could still form one independent state or one canton. Many countries, including the United States and the United Kingdom, are not made up of a single unbroken area.

Whatever the case, the homelands and national states should be free to decide whether to join the canton system or become independent.

CHAPTER 12

Problems Arising from a Canton System

Life in its own journey, presupposes its own change and movement, and one tries to arrest them at one's eternal peril.

— Laurens Van der Post

Unequal Wealth

MANY PEOPLE FEAR THAT, because some cantons will inevitably be wealthier than others, this will lead to friction. But these disparities between states occur in all countries. Regional differences do not cause conflict as long as there is freedom of movement, so that a person does not have to live in a poor canton. Poor cantons may have other attributes—geography, climate, culture, traditions, economic system, personal freedom, or whatever—that their citizens value more highly than material wealth.

It is important to note that people do not always migrate from rural to urban areas, small to big towns, poor to rich areas. The latest U.S. census, for example, revealed a net migration the other way. There have also been mass migrations from richer to poorer countries. People most commonly migrate to places where there is more personal freedom and opportunity, or higher growth, than they are currently experiencing.

Is it not possible, then, that this tendency, combined with freedom of movement, will result in overcrowding of cantons that enjoy high levels of freedom, opportunity, and growth? The point to consider here is whether "overcrowding" is indeed a problem. The population of Hong Kong increased by four million in two decades. Newcomers, who usually arrive with nothing, move into transitional slums, then quickly move out to better areas as they take advantage of the free economy and begin to produce and prosper.

Policies that aim to control the movement of people from one area to another are, in any case, largely ineffective. Soweto has an official population of 800,000, but estimates place the de facto population at somewhere between 1.7 and 2 million. In other words, there are more people living illegally in Soweto than legally. Clearly, influx control did not keep people out of Soweto, and now that it has been abolished, chances are the size of its population will not alter very much. Those who move to Soweto, or anywhere else, do so because they believe they will be better off.

In South West Africa/Namibia, influx control and group areas laws were abolished nearly a decade ago. A few black professionals and politicians moved into white areas. A few hundred blacks settled in a squatter camp on the periphery of Katachura (a black township outside Windhoek). But after a year or so this camp returned to its former size. The truth is that barriers to movement are harmful. They cause uncertainty, hostility, resentment, and conflict among the people they affect; promote abuse; and reduce economic efficiency.

Some will argue that, even given free movement, it is not fair that some cantons should have rich mineral deposits or agricultural lands while others have nothing. We have tried to show that transferring wealth through taxation or by any other method does a great deal more harm than good. However, if people remain unconvinced and vote for some form of redistribution, one way of doing this would be to allow the central government to tax profits on natural resources and redistribute this wealth throughout the federation in the form of infrastructure such as roads, or in vouchers for education, medical services, and so on. This idea is discussed at greater length in Chapter 15.

Viability

Some people believe that for a canton or state to be "viable" as an autonomous unit, it must be big or rich. This is simply not so. Many sovereign countries are tiny in size or population, and many others have negligible per capita incomes or natural resources. Of the 188 countries listed in the 1980 *Book of Rankings*, six have an area of less than ten square miles; over thirty have less than 1,000 square miles. Ten countries have fewer than 30,000 citizens, and approximately twenty have populations of less than 100,000. Monaco and Liechtenstein each have only 25,000 people, Greenland 51,000, Bermuda 58,000, Seychelles 61,000, Tonga 92,000, and Grenada 108,000. By comparison, the average magisterial district in South Africa has 80,000 people.

Of the 145 countries for which figures are available, fully thirty show an estimated per capita gross national product of less than $200. Over half the countries have per capita GNPs estimated at under $1,000. The South African average in 1980 was $1,340. Thus even the most depressed districts in this country are well above the national average in many countries that are considered viable.

Does Diversity Cause Confusion?

If many cantons function autonomously, will this lead to a troublesome lack of uniformity in matters of mutual interest such as road rules, railway gauges, and electrical voltages? As bylaws change from one municipality to the next, will this create confusion and will there be an unnecessary duplication of services such as trash collection, electrical power generation, public transportation, and higher education?

The answer to these questions is no.

In Switzerland, the federal government may build a highway across the country only with the consent of every canton through which it will run. However, this does not stop highways from being built. Also, history shows that standards tend to emerge wherever they serve people's interests. North America provides a classic illustration of a privately owned and run railway network being standardized through many autonomous states and provinces without any government-imposed standards or laws. When the railway companies had difficulty in operating through different time zones, they adopted the standardized time zones that still apply in North America today.

Furthermore, South Africa already has relative uniformity in areas such as currency, weights and measures, and health laws, although it is interesting to note that we do not have uniformity in many areas in which one would expect it. For example, traffic regulations vary between provinces and between local governments within provinces. There are three different government railway gauges in addition to the variety of gauges used by the private sector at mines and factory sites. Pretoria and Johannesburg have different electricity voltages and cycles.

Bylaws regarding swimming pool fences, buildings, cemeteries, outdoor advertising, property taxes, and so on already vary from one municipality to the next. The homelands have different tax rates, labor laws, licensing procedures, and land tenure regulations. None of these variations creates confusion.

Most countries in the world impose uniform standards in some areas and permit diversity in others for no more than random historical reasons. Many diversify where we standardize or standardize where we allow differences.

It is sometimes argued that a uniform economic policy should be imposed by the central government on the whole country, because if one area deregulates and imposes low taxes it gains an unfair advantage over others. However, in a canton system there is nothing to stop cantons that are disadvantaged in this manner from following suit and achieving equal advantages for themselves. In both the United States and Switzerland there are some states or cantons that have relatively high taxes and others where taxes are very low. Obviously, people trade off the advantages of a given economic policy against other factors.

We propose that central government be prevented by the constitution from imposing standards on the whole country, because imposed uniformity in a heterogeneous society inevitably leads to inappropriate policies for many groups.

Unregulated markets have a remarkable tendency to provide the best solutions for most people's needs. Spontaneous standardization occurs where it is in the consumer's interest — even in such seemingly unimportant matters as baby bottle tops or stone crushers. On the other hand, where standardization impedes innovation, the market jettisons it. Consumers vote with their rands or dollars for variety or uniformity as suits their needs. Similarly, in a canton system they would vote through referendums, or with their feet, for variety or uniformity in the provision of infrastructure and services. Also, as we have mentioned, wherever it proved convenient, cantons or communities could cooperate to provide amenities or to contract for services with private enterprises.

Problems Resulting from Freedom of Movement

It is easy to talk about the freedom of people to leave cantons whose political or economic system they do not like, and move to more congenial areas. But this will cause considerable disruption, hardship, and loss of wealth. A white farmer working and living on land that has been in his family for generations will not be greatly comforted by the knowledge that if he does not like the local policy of racial integration, he can sell his farm and move.

But South Africa is on the verge of great change, and change by its very nature will cause disruption. Moreover, black people have never enjoyed security of tenure and have been evicted from their land and forcibly moved without a second thought on the part of successive governments. The current political unrest and economic recession have already caused great suffering, and this will be escalated by any attempt to prolong the status quo. If we do not implement a solution that is acceptable to all racial groups, a bloody revolution could be followed by a Marxist state in which the opportunity to sell one's property and move voluntarily would seem heaven-sent.

Once a canton system is introduced, there will be an inevita-

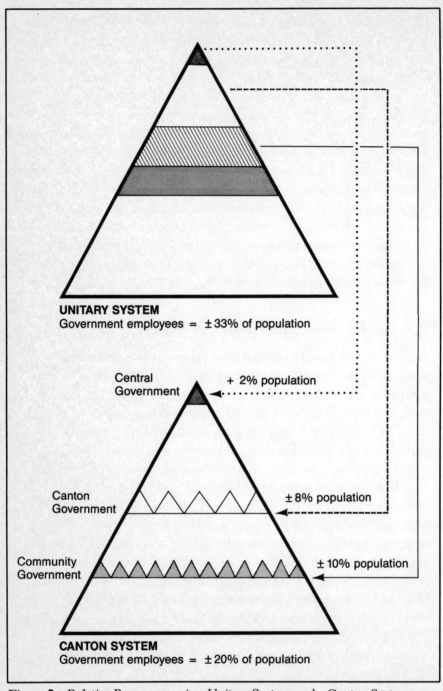

UNITARY SYSTEM
Government employees = ±33% of population

Central Government   + 2% population

Canton Government   ±8% population

Community Government   ±10% population

CANTON SYSTEM
Government employees = ±20% of population

Figure 2   Relative Bureaucracy in a Unitary System and a Canton System

ble period of readjustment while boundaries get established and people gravitate to more congenial areas, but this will create a fraction of the disruption that would result from any of the other alternatives currently facing the country.

Bureaucratization

One might expect that with a multiplicity of governments there will be a massive increase in bureaucracy. In truth, however, when government is devolved there are usually fewer rather than more civil servants. In proportion to population, Switzerland has the smallest civil service in Europe, the lowest tax rates, and the smallest budget, despite having the greatest proliferation of governments.

The reason for this is both simple and exciting.

When a government is highly centralized, a pyramid of bureaucratic management structures is created, with many tiers between central and local government. Every senior official has several others under him, and this occurs all the way down to the lowest level. In a decentralized government, the upper part of the pyramid falls away, leaving only the base. (See Fig. 2).

Does a Canton System
Need a Sophisticated Population?

It is sometimes suggested that a canton system is suitable only for a society that has reached Switzerland's level of sophistication, and would therefore not work well in South Africa. Remember, however, that the Swiss system originated in the thirteenth century; the first three cantons were "forest cantons" whose residents were in many ways less sophisticated than South Africa's "Third World" sector.

Second, the black tribal authorities in South Africa already operate very much as cantons or communities do. There are some eighty tribal authorities in Transkei, over forty in Ciskei, and about one-hundred in Bophuthatswana. They are small local governments usually made up of traditional rural people who know their own community needs. They debate and discuss issues in the village square, or *indaba*, just as the people in the small Swiss cantons and communities do. If anything, the simpler the structure of a community, the more appropriate a maximally devolved system becomes.

In truth a canton system is even more appropriate for South Africa than it is for Switzerland.

CHAPTER 13

Central Government in a Canton System

. . . Apartheid has to go and it has to be replaced with a social and political system which will give both black and white a meaningful stake in the government of their country.
— Chief Mangosuthu G. Buthelezi

CANTON PARLIAMENTS OR ASSEMBLIES constitute the most important level of government in our proposal, and therefore we have discussed them first. Now let us turn to the central government and consider what its functions should be and how it would relate to the cantons.

The central government should be seen not so much as a governing body as an agency for the protection of cantons and the basic rights of its citizens. It should promote cooperation between canton governments and should be administrative rather than legislative in character.

The national constitution should be based on two main principles: maximal devolution and strict limitation of central government power. The implementation of these principles would be assisted by the following provisos:

1. There must be an unambiguous separation of judicial, administrative, and legislative functions. The judiciary should have power

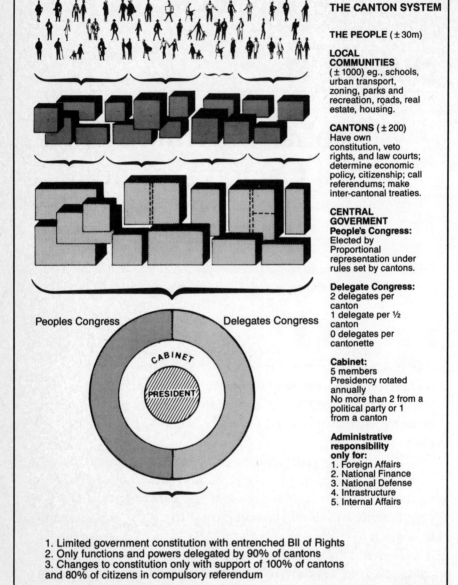

THE CANTON SYSTEM

THE PEOPLE (± 30m)

LOCAL COMMUNITIES
(± 1000) eg., schools, urban transport, zoning, parks and recreation, roads, real estate, housing.

CANTONS (± 200)
Have own constitution, veto rights, and law courts; determine economic policy, citizenship; call referendums; make inter-cantonal treaties.

CENTRAL GOVERMENT
People's Congress:
Elected by Proportional representation under rules set by cantons.

Delegate Congress:
2 delegates per canton
1 delegate per ½ canton
0 delegates per cantonette

Cabinet:
5 members
Presidency rotated annually
No more than 2 from a political party or 1 from a canton

Administrative responsibility only for:
1. Foreign Affairs
2. National Finance
3. National Defense
4. Intrastructure
5. Internal Affairs

Peoples Congress   Delegates Congress

CABINET

PRESIDENT

1. Limited government constitution with entrenched BIl of Rights
2. Only functions and powers delegated by 90% of cantons
3. Changes to constitution only with support of 100% of cantons and 80% of citizens in compulsory referendum

Figure 3   The Canton System

to override any unconstitutional action by central government.

2. Any additional powers and functions that can be effectively devolved to cantons or communities should not be exercised by the central government unless agreed upon by, say, 90 percent of all the cantons.

3. To avoid domination of minorities, amendments to the constitution should require endorsement by each canton at a constitutional convention. (If one canton keeps vetoing an amendment that all the others support, it can be threatened with expulsion.)

4. Central government must not be able to subsidize constituent units in order to centralize power. States, provinces, or districts must not be bribed by central government into accepting certain regulations in exchange for grants.

Structure

As in Switzerland, the United States, and elsewhere, the central government should consist of two houses of equal status, plus a cabinet. These would be constituted in such a way so as to avoid as far as possible the potential for bad government, regardless of who governs.

The People's Congress

With the proviso that there should be at least one representative from each canton, representation in the first house would be on the basis of population. It would be the direct representative of the people by proportional representation.

South Africans are used to the Westminster system inherited from Britain. Under this system, candidates run as independents or for political parties in constituencies or wards. It is hypothetically possible for a single party to receive 51 percent of the votes in every constituency. It would thus win 100 percent of the seats in Parliament despite having only the barest majority of supporters. It is not uncommon under the Westminster system for a party to win a majority of constituencies even though it has received a minority of votes. This usually happens when urban constituencies are loaded so that rural votes carry more weight.

The Westminster system is unusual. More commonly, countries have opted for proportional representation. Political parties or geographic units are represented in government in proportion to the number of voters. If there are, say, three parties that win votes in the ratio of 60:30:10, they will have representatives in roughly that ratio.

Proportional representation can take various forms but tends to fall into two main categories. One option is for representation to be based on population density. In the canton system, this would mean that a canton with a million voters would have twice as many representatives as one with 500,000, ten times as many as a canton with 100,000, and so on. The second option is for each political party to have proportional representation based on the number of votes cast nationwide in its favor.

We suggest the former system for a number of reasons. In order to depoliticize central government and reduce intergroup hostility, it is important that party politics be primarily a canton affair. There may be a handful of parties that are represented in all cantons. But technically, although they have central bodies and the same name and policies, they should be separate canton parties constituting a national movement. The whole object of devolving power to autonomous geographic units is to ensure that minorities are not swamped. Representation based on national political parties would probably lead to entire populations having no representation in the People's Congress. This is because some political parties in South Africa represent small but important minorities, such as Indians or Coloureds and black and white separatist groups. It is essential that these minorities be represented in both houses of the central government.

Representation based on canton population is likely to reflect party proportionality. Cantons would be free to elect their representatives on any basis, including those of proportions based on party support.

It is likely that some cantons would not qualify for representation on the basis of population. We therefore suggest that each canton, regardless of size, be entitled to at least one representative in the People's Congress.

The Delegates' Congress

The second house would be composed of two delegates from each canton regardless of size. Should a canton split into two parts, each would send one delegate. If further splintering occurred and part-cantons or "cantonettes" were formed, they would enjoy the same autonomy as other cantons but would forfeit their right to representation in the Delegates' Congress. This would prevent pseudo-cantons from forming merely in order to dominate the Delegates' Congress.

This formula of one house with proportional representation and another based on equal representation avoids the risk of group domination and works very well in other countries where the case for it is less compelling than in South Africa.

So long as ethnic consciousness and identification survive, both houses may be expected to have black majorities. The People's Congress will probably reflect the numerical relationship between the major population groups: about 72 percent black, 16 percent white, 9 percent Coloured, and 3 percent Asian. The various black groups (Zulus, Xhosas, Sothos, etc.) may also be represented on a roughly proportional basis, depending on how people vote.

Until the initial delimitation has taken place, we have no way of knowing how many cantons will have black majorities, but it is likely that most will. Thus the Delegates' Congress would probably also have a black majority. In every sense South Africa would have "black majority government" and "one person, one vote"— or, more precisely, "one adult, many votes." But there would be an adequate set of checks and balances to prevent black majority "dictatorship."

The smaller rural cantons would have a majority in the Delegates' Congress, and they would tend to be moderate or conservative regardless of race. The major metropolitan cantons, which would have a majority in the People's Congress, would probably be more radical. The two would balance each other, much as the House of Representatives and Senate do in the United States. Moderate minorities would rely on the Delegates to preserve their values and interests to the extent that they are not already protected by the Bill of Rights, the degree of local community autonomy, intercanton autonomy, and the other factors we will mention in Chapter 14.

The Cabinet and Central Government Departments

To ensure maximal depoliticization of central government, we propose that the central government be responsible for only five areas of central administration, each with one presiding minister. The five ministers would constitute the Cabinet. They would be elected by both houses sitting together in the Joint National Congress. The cabinet ministers could be chosen from any canton and any political party, provided that each minister is from a different canton and not more than two belong to the same political party.

The Joint National Congress would elect one of the ministers each year, and for one year only, to chair cabinet meetings. He would be the National President. His duties would be purely administrative, and would include matters of protocol.

The five central government departments would have the usual responsibilities as follows:

1. Foreign Affairs: international relations, immigration, diplomatic corps.

2. Finance: central budget, import and excise duties, currency, mint, foreign exchange, reserve bank.

3. Defense: protection against foreign invasion and civil war, emergency relief.

4. Infrastructure: national roads, railways, power supply, pipelines. (This department would place infrastructure — roads and railways, for example — only in cantons that give their consent, as in Switzerland.)

5. Internal Affairs: registration of births, marriages, and deaths, population distribution, national statistical services, appeals courts, environment, functions delegated by cantons.

"Treaty" Functions of Central Government

In addition to the five primary functions, the central government would have secondary or "treaty" functions delegated to it by cantons, in much the same way that the ex-protectorates and homelands have arranged for the Republic of South Africa government to do certain things for them. These might range from administering a customs and monetary union to providing transport services and registrars of financial institutions.

Initially, many cantons and communities would be unprepared to take on various responsibilities. They could arrange for the central government to perform these functions for them until they are ready to do so, or indefinitely. As a rule, delegated functions would go to the Department of Internal Affairs and Regional Services Councils. Alternatively, arrangements could be made between cantons, or between communities, or with private companies. Every situation will suggest an appropriate solution, and provided one starts from a position of maximal devolution, the optimal amount of centralization will come about spontaneously.

Citizenship

Everyone will have dual or treble citizenship, as each individual will be a citizen of the country, a canton, and possibly a community as well. National citizenship will be automatic and immediate for present South Africans and homeland citizens. Citizenship of cantons or communities will be subject to canton policy and procedures.

Voting

In most cantons there will be "one adult, many votes." People will vote in their communities on community issues, in cantons on canton issues, and in national referendums on national issues. Some cantons might have authoritarian governments that make unilateral decisions without involving the citizens. The citizens of such a canton would have the constitutional right to call a referendum on an unpopular measure, to oust the canton government, or to amend its constitution as outlined in our discussion on the Bill of Rights (see Appendix I).

Depoliticization

With maximal devolution to canton level, there would be very little contact between citizens and central government. Citizens would not vote directly for the central government, nor would they be directly taxed by it. Any contact would be purely administrative and confined to matters that do not provoke conflict. For example, a person might deal with a central customs officer, or register his child's birth or his marriage at a central agency, but this would not provide any basis for dispute or hostility between groups.

The majority of people in the central government would certainly be black, but this would not mean that Indians, Coloureds, whites, Chinese, Japanese, Jews, Moslems, Hindus, or Buddhists would be ruled by blacks, because the central government would not have the power to impose its policies or values on anyone.

Defense

Some people fear that if central government controls defense and blacks constitute a majority in central government, they will use the army to seize power and create a black one-party state.

This fear is based on the assumption that the majority of cantons would be dominated by the same political party and that this party would want to dominate the entire country. There is no evidence to support this assumption. Opinion surveys indicate that black support is split among a number of different groups, none of which attains anything approaching a majority. Cantonization would probably result in the formation of even more political groups representing local interests. Surveys also indicate that the majority of blacks are moderate. They want economic freedom and political representation, but few nurse a desire for revenge or retribution. We discuss this in greater depth in Chapter 14. Even the relatively radical groups with strong support, the ANC and UDF, favor minority rights and power-sharing.

The fear of a black military coup is also based on the assumption that blacks will not be happy with the way things will be. In a canton system they would have both freedom and the power to control their own lives. There would be no incentive to risk civil war in order to remove rights of whites, Coloureds, and Indians that don't infringe their own rights, or to risk chasing away white capital, investment, and expertise. The black political groups that propose controlling the entire country and nationalizing all wealth have such a small following that they pose no real threat.

There would be citizens of all the cantons in the armed forces, and the canton governments would decide whether servicemen should be volunteers or conscripts. Alternatively, the cantons might decide on a system whereby each runs its own army and contributes, as the European countries do to NATO, to a National Defense Alliance. Under such a system, if war broke out between two or more cantons the Defense Alliance of the remaining cantons could still be called in to restore peace.

Racial Discrimination

Whether people should or should not be allowed to discriminate—or, indeed, should be *forced* to discriminate—on racial grounds is a highly emotionally charged and conflict-provoking issue.

We suggest two alternatives:

Our preference is for a constitutionally entrenched prohibition on discrimination by government at all levels. In other words, government would be colorblind—entirely nonracial. Any law that results in any form of compulsory integration or segregation would be unconstitutional. But if someone wanted to establish a trade union with black members only, or a school open to Jews only, or a swimming pool reserved for women only, or a theater open to all— all of these options would be legal, provided they are voluntarily and privately financed.

Thus all citizens would have the right to integrate or to segregate voluntarily at their own expense, but it would be unconstitutional for any level of government to enforce integration or segregation, or to discriminate, for example, in its employment practices or the provision of public facilities.

The general constitutional prohibition on discrimination would be supported by a number of entrenched clauses in the Bill of Rights regarding equality before the law, freedom of movement, freedom of association and disassociation, and property rights.

The second alternative would be to include a "sunset clause" in the constitution allowing local communities or cantons to maintain racial laws for ten years. This alternative would mean that the thorough protection of individual rights our system offers would become fully effective only when the sunset clause lapsed. Up to that date, cantons and communities could maintain existing race laws, relax them, or abolish them. We offer this alternative because a significant number of South Africans, mostly white Afrikaners, but also members of other population groups, are determined to maintain racial segregation.

This approach would give cantons or communities controlled by white nationalists breathing space in which to buy up land so that, when the sunset clause lapses, they could exclude unwanted people from their areas by exercising their property rights. "Whites only" cantons could be created in a number of ways. Racial separatists could make representations to the Delimitation Commission for the creation of an adequate number of cantons in areas where there already are, or could relatively easily be, a majority of whites. To the extent they did not succeed at the delimitation stage, they could organize a popular initiative and create white majority cantons through referendums. These could be consolidated by purchasing land. In order to refuse entry to blacks in "whites only" cantons, they would have to buy all the land in their cantons or communities. They would not, however, be able to prevent people who are not white from using national roads.

White nationalists would take the risk, however, that such an extreme degree of voluntary discrimination might be so offensive to the majority of cantons that the expulsion procedure might be initiated or threatened against them. It might simply be unacceptable to blacks, who will constitute a majority in most cantons. Nonetheless, we believe that the system we propose gives white nationalists the only realistic prospect of indulging their racial preference indefinitely in a manner that could gain international and local acceptance, even though frowned upon. Conversely, there is no realistic prospect that statutory apartheid can be sustained in the long term.

However, if racial nationalists are not convinced, our system still leaves them with the option of secession. If separatist cantons secede, they will become sovereign countries, free to do as they choose. They would be taking it upon themselves to face the wrath of the world, but without forcing the rest of the country to suffer from international condemnation.

The sunset clause would also allow black nationalist governments in areas such as Soweto to refuse entry to white businesses in order to give black businessmen a chance to make up for historical disadvantages. The influential black chamber of commerce movement, NAFCOC, favors a policy along these lines.

The canton system would produce its own dynamic, spontaneous order and process, the results of which cannot be forecast with accuracy. But our guess is that there will be such a massive de-escalation of racial tensions and conflict that even those groups that now exhibit seemingly boundless racial hostility will be mollified.

For this country to have any prospect of enduring peace and prosperity all the major groupings need to see light at the end of the tunnel in terms of their own interests. It is highly unlikely that any of them will attain their stated goals on a national scale. The best they can hope for is to do so in the limited spheres of influence permitted by a canton system.

CHAPTER 14

Protection of Minorities

During my lifetime . . . I have fought against white domination, and I have fought against black domination. I have cherished the ideal of a democratic and free society in which all persons live together in harmony and with equal opportunities. It is an ideal which I hope to live for and achieve. But if needs be, it is an ideal for which I am prepared to die.

—Nelson Mandela, 1964

APPROXIMATELY 72 PERCENT of South Africans are black, 16 percent white, 9 percent Coloured, and 3 percent Asian.

The large black majority causes most whites, and many Indians and Coloureds, to fear a winner-take-all political system with universal suffrage. They are afraid that blacks will impose a system that does not recognize minority interests, or that there will be "one person, one vote"—once. Only a canton system such as we have outlined in the preceding chapters allows for universal suffrage and complete equality of every individual before the law, within a structure that protects minority rights in many different ways.

What are Minority Rights?

Minority rights may be defined as the rights a minority requires to live according to its common values. Minorities are individuals with

South Africa's Minorities

Blacks:	72%			Whites:	16%
Zulu	21%	Ndebele	2%	Afrikaans-speaking	10%
Xhosa	19%	Swazi	2%	English-speaking	6%
Sotho	13%	Venda	2%		
Tswana	9%	Others	1%	Coloureds:	9%
Tsonga	3%			Indians:	3%

common interests or values not shared by the majority. In South Africa, minorities include not only whites, Indians, and Coloureds, but also Xhosas, Afrikaners, Jews, South Sothos, Muslims, old people, the unemployed, foreigners, homosexuals, the handicapped, and lefthanded people.

Ultimately, every individual has a unique set of interests and values, and is therefore a minority. Stated differently, there are not minorities or majorities, but only individuals with interests they share with a few or many other individuals. Thus, if individual rights are adequately protected, the rights of minorities and majorities will also be protected.

We have seen that in the course of South Africa's history white minority rights were not only protected but were artificially advanced by gross violations of blacks', Coloureds', and Indians' rights. Laws were passed not just to protect white rights, but to safeguard white privilege. Most whites, including the present government, are now prepared to phase out the vast body of discriminatory laws and policies that has been built up over the last 330 years. But the fear of black domination—the "swart gevaar"—remains the major stumbling block.

The "Swart Gevaar"

What most whites fear is that, given unlimited and centralized political power of the kind whites have held and abused, blacks will evict whites from their homes, nationalize their businesses, and loot their property in an orgy of redistribution and revenge. But there is a good deal of evidence to suggest that this danger is more imagined than real.

True, there are many articulate political leaders who speak openly about the day of reckoning when AZAPO would restore the land to its "original owners," or the ANC would return it to "those who work it." A handful would like to see a full-fledged Marxist dictatorship with no private property at all. But the majority of blacks seem to want no more than the removal of all barriers to black advancement and enfranchisement.

Many people point to the rest of Africa to justify their fear of black domination. They look at the socialist dictatorship of such one-party states as Zaire, Tanzania, Ethiopia, and Angola, and argue that there, but for white control, go they—into an abyss of poverty and mismanagement.

To be fair, we should observe that this is not universally true. Botswana is a real multiparty democracy. In Swaziland, white farmers own well over half the land and enjoy full property rights under a black government. The Ivory Coast is a capitalist economic success story. Kenya has heterogeneous harmony. Increasingly, black African countries have turned to the West for advice and support. In addition, South African blacks are more sophisticated, better educated, and have higher living standards than the vast majority in the rest of Africa.

Evidence suggests that the assumption that voting would be along ethnic, linguistic, and cultural lines may be mistaken. There may be stronger ideological alignments. Various surveys have been conducted to assess the relative support for different political groups. While findings vary, it seems that many people who are not Zulus nonetheless support Inkatha, and many people other than Xhosas support the ANC. One survey even indicated a large following for President P. W. Botha among blacks. It seems that the majority of blacks would support some kind of moderate alliance (see Appendix II).

None of the four independent homelands has adopted the policies whites fear most. They have repealed all race laws, but none has espoused Marxism. Bophuthatswana and Ciskei have recently taken major steps to free their economies. All four have been more financially responsible than the South African government.

In his book *Permanent Peace,* which we highly recommend, Denis Beckett describes the type of black leader that might be expected to emerge in a typical small rural town with a population of around 50,000, of which over 90 percent are black. He points out that the whites are barely aware of the existence of the people who enjoy distinction in the eyes of the local black community:

> Foremost of these is the principal chief in the area, one Kelly Molete. Chief Molete is a middle-aged man, a committed Christian and university graduate of considerable sophistication, well endowed with charm and old-world courtesy.
>
> There is also a prominent businessman, Khumalo, a man of Zulu stock who lived in the area for years with his Zuluness never an issue until recently, when the rise of Tswana ethnicity induced by the creation of Bophuthatswana has tended to accentuate his outside origins. His farming activities and brickworks nonetheless make him the major black work-provider in the district and he is generally well thought of.
>
> There is a lawyer named Absolom Motleleng, who is the nominal AZAPO presence in the area. He is about thirty years old and after some time in Johannesburg recently returned to his home district to set up a practice there. His maroon BMW is well known to the people of the townships.
>
> There is also one Phaka, a one-time farmworker from Ventersdorp who lost both home and job when his employer decided he was a trouble-maker. He was dispatched to a resettlement camp which borders on and overlaps with Chief Molete's land. There he has by force of personality, and with the backup of a crew of henchmen who are, according to viewpoint, either the sustainers of local order or a gang of toughs, established a position of dominance.

Beckett shows that these are real people, known to him and representative of typical black community leaders. When these black leaders approach the local white town council to discuss a new dispensation, they do so *en bloc* because they are bound by common interests. However, Khumalo is dedicated to free enterprise, Molete is not very interested in economics but wants to do his best for his tribe, and Motleleng, while theoretically committed to socialism, is in practice concerned about peace and stability and improving the quality of life of blacks. Phaka is excluded from the delegation:

> In the first place, he will have none of this parleying with the boere. He has his fiefdom, and he perceives black power as on the horizon with the declared constitutional changes. He'll wait and he'll make his run a little further along the road, when he can see the opening to power that counts, not just petty Sannieshof power. In the second place, there

is no way that Chief Molete is going to have Phaka sitting on any delegation that he leads. Phaka is a thorn in his flesh. He considers him an upstart and a nuisance, and the organization which Phaka runs in the squatter township is a major disruption to Molete's tribe.

Beckett continues:

> The traditional white idea of the black bogeyman waiting to take over the country . . . a red-hot Africanist and a communist and an anarchist all at the same time . . . does not actually exist in any single person, least of all one with leadership pretensions. The Africanists and the communists tend to be quite drastically at loggerheads with one another, with the Africanists such as they are being also thoroughly divided among themselves over their attitude to the rights of whites, and the only true anarchists are a few white middleclass intellectual mavericks. The teenage township stone-throwers who are alleged to be anarchists are really the resentful flotsam which a hopeless political structure such as ours inevitably throws up.

Even if all the evidence we have presented is invalid, and many blacks in fact harbor a desire for revenge or an urge to plunder, the system we propose offers many effective protections for minorities.

Entrenched Minority Protection

All the safeguards listed here are discussed in detail elsewhere. We repeat them only in order to highlight the extent of protection they afford minorities.

The proposed Bill of Rights includes the following entrenched provisions specifically intended to protect individual, and thus minority, rights:

1. **Freedom of movement:** This would enable people to leave cantons whose policies did not concur with their own values, and move to more congenial ones.

2. **Property rights:** The fundamental right of all people to own and acquire property is supplemented by an anti-expropriation clause, a proprietal rights clause, and a nominative boundary clause. The anti-expropriation clause would prevent government from expropriating land for any reason other than the provision of infrastructure, and would ensure that there is proper compensation in such cases. The proprietal rights clause

would protect the right of a property owner or proprietor to admit or exclude anyone, regardless of his reason, to or from his property. The nominative boundary clause would enable property owners living on canton boundaries to apply for inclusion in whichever canton they prefer. This would be particularly useful for farmers.

3. **The right to associate and disassociate:** This ensures the freedom of individuals to fraternize with or separate from whomever they wish, and would render compulsory integration unconstitutional.

4. **The right to call for referendums:** When government officials abuse their office, people could launch popular initiatives through which they could call for a new election, request inclusion in another canton, or have any unpopular measure withdrawn. Within black majority cantons, spheres of white, Indian, or Coloured majority influence could be created by establishing semi-cantons or cantonettes and by negotiating for maximal autonomy in local, predominantly white, Coloured, or Indian communities or towns.

5. **Victimization of minorities:** Any minority would be able to bring a court action against a government measure amounting to the abuse of majority power for the purpose of victimizing the minority.

6. **Intimidation:** Intimidation would be a major offense so that the moderate majority would have effective protection and be free to pursue their interests without fear.

The entire structure of the canton system is based on the idea of returning decision making to the people. We have discussed how political competition between cantons and the "demonstration effect" discipline canton governments to act in the interests of their residents.

Ultimately, the only way to avoid group domination is by allowing people to govern themselves. Given self-government, even without all the constitutional safeguards we have included, we can safely rely on the most meaningful protection of all: the goodwill of most South Africans—black, white, Indian, and Coloured alike.

CHAPTER 15

Socioeconomic Solutions

All people shall have equal rights to trade where they choose, to manufacture and to enter all trades, crafts and professions.

— The ANC Freedom Charter

THROUGHOUT THIS BOOK we have put the case for a free South African society, a society with maximal individual autonomy and responsibility and minimal government intervention. We have suggested that central government in South Africa should be confined to five areas of control: foreign affairs, finance, defense, infrastructure, and internal affairs. Canton governments should control all other aspects of government in their own areas.

In this chapter, we consider some of the socioeconomic functions of central, canton, and community government in more detail. We also suggest ways in which education and welfare might be provided more satisfactorily, and we list economic measures the present government should undertake immediately in order to de-escalate conflict.

Canton Powers

Most economic policy decisions would be made at canton and community government levels. Provided they comply with the Bill of

Rights, cantons would be free to pursue any economic policy. They would have, for example, their own company laws and deeds registry laws, and their own policies regarding tax, welfare, housing, agriculture, licensing, standards, health, education, and so on.

South Africa's political groups have conflicting views on economic policy. But at present the competition between them is confined to largely theoretical arguments. In a canton system, there would be a visible and lively contest between their differing views. We would see through practical demonstration which policies produce the best results.

Taxation in a Canton System

In the system proposed in this book, central government would have no power to tax citizens directly, nor would it be empowered to redistribute wealth or subsidize cantons. The relatively small amount of revenue required to finance its own administrative functions would come primarily from foreign trade in the form of customs duties, export earnings, excise duties, or tariffs, as agreed by the cantons. Income would also be generated by user charges such as tolls on national roads and court fees for supreme and appeals courts.

With the unanimous agreement of the cantons, revenue might be raised for central government through an annual canton tax based on population. For example, each canton might pay to central government R100 ($50) per citizen for the following budget year. Cantons could finance this in their own way. Each canton would have its own taxation policy, and it would soon become evident which policies achieved the best results.

Economic theory shows that, when taxes are raised higher than about 25 percent of GNP, the effect on the economy is so counterproductive that revenue collected is less than it would have been if taxes had been kept down. This has been demonstrated in Ciskei, where a flat tax rate of 15 percent has been introduced, with the first R8,000 of income being tax free. Some 90 percent of Ciskeians in the lower income bracket no longer pay tax, but early evidence suggests that, as a result of an influx of industries and capital, Ciskei will gather more revenue than it did previously under the South

African tax structure. Ciskei also held sales tax at 10 percent instead of raising it to 12 percent as did South Africa, and monthly returns show an increase of more than 50 percent in revenue from sales tax. Ciskei is currently experiencing an annual growth rate of around 8 percent, compared to South Africa's 2 percent.

Until this century, there were no income or corporate taxes in most countries of the world, and governments got along very well without them. They were introduced mainly during World War I as a temporary war measure.* Unfortunately, they remain with us.

Transportation

All South Africa's transport services — sea, road, rail, and air — were started by private enterprise under free market conditions. For various reasons, under different governments and at different times all of these have been nationalized or heavily regulated. Many people now subscribe to the myth that the state had to undertake these activities because the private sector could or would not.

One of the primary reasons for transport regulations has been to keep blacks, Indians, and Coloureds out of the transportation sector. During the nineteenth century, blacks discovered what they know today: that one of the easiest entry points to the economy is through transportation. "I can well call to mind the time when, with only one or two exceptions, there were no wagons in Kaffraria but those belonging to Europeans; now, however, native wagons are so plentiful as to be quite a nuisance."[1]

In the late 1800s, most "transport riders" responsible for conveying people and goods thousands of miles across southern Africa were blacks. Today there is apparently not a single black licensed truck operator in South Africa. The handful of blacks who do have road haulage permits are not using them because there is no demand on the routes for which they are authorized. The effect of restrictive transport licensing has been to ensure that virtually all licenses

---

*Personal income tax was not introduced in South Africa until 1914, and company tax (apart from a very low tax of about 5 percent on gold and diamond mining activities) was not introduced until 1925.

have gone to government-owned or private white-owned transport monopolies. Perhaps no other area demonstrates as unambiguously as transport does that government interference with the market is conflict-provoking and politicizing.

The deregulation of transport in general, and of black urban transport in particular, would not only help defuse unrest in the townships, but would also provide thousands of job opportunities for blacks. Men and women can become taxi drivers with little education and training, and with no more money than is needed to pay for a driver's license and a deposit on a vehicle.

The government is currently pouring hundreds of millions of rands into ill-conceived job creation and small business development programs, at great net cost to the economy as a whole. It could achieve a great deal more by the simple expedient of drawing a line through the Road Transportation Act.

South Africa is one of the few countries outside the communist bloc that has a totally centralized and uniform transport policy. In most countries, urban transport policy is devolved to local governments, and regional transport to states or provinces, while central government controls only national transport. Whether or not South Africa is cantonized, a policy of this kind should be pursued.

In the canton system we propose, central government would not have the power to regulate transport. Each canton would have its own transport policy, and many would probably deregulate transport or devolve transport policy to communities. This would prevent the following kind of incident from occurring.

In 1979 a company called City Mini Cabs applied to the Transportation Board for a permit to run 100 cruising taxis in Johannesburg. South African cities have possibly the worst taxi services in the world. There are very few taxis in proportion to population and they are hard to identify. They may not cruise, nor may they be hailed in the streets; they must wait at taxi stands for clients to come to them or call for them by telephone. The situation is so bad that at one time the American trade consul felt constrained to produce a pamphlet explaining to visiting Americans why they would have difficulty finding taxis in South Africa.

City Mini Cabs seemed to have an open-and-shut case. Their permit application was argued at great cost by experienced lawyers and supported by the Johannesburg Municipality, the Central Business District Association, the Free Market Foundation, and the Chamber of Commerce. It was turned down by the Transportation Board.

If Johannesburg controlled its own urban transport, City Mini Cabs' application would have been granted, along with many others. The same applies to cities and towns all over the country.

Transport specialist Terry Markman estimates that the full cost to the South African economy of transport regulation exceeds R1 billion ($500 million) per annum. Deregulation and privatization would make the country R1 billion richer, provide small business opportunities for many thousands of blacks, depoliticize one of the most conflict-ridden areas of the economy, provide greatly improved services to the community, and reduce traffic congestion, because more people would use urban transport instead of private cars.

Agriculture

Several important changes should be made in South Africa's agricultural sector, which, like transport, would be controlled at the canton level in our system.

The rigid agricultural controls that handicap farmers should be phased out and all attempts to keep uneconomic farmers on the land should be discontinued. This would mean that large tracts of underused and overused farm land would come onto the market at about the same time that legislation preventing blacks from buying land is abolished. Blacks with insufficient capital to purchase land could initially become tenant farmers. The few successful black commercial farmers who have emerged in recent years are mostly farmers in the homelands who have leased farms from tribal authorities, the homeland development corporations, or the Development Trust (the single biggest landholder in South Africa).

Since blacks have been denied experience in real estate markets, many do not realize that very little up-front capital is required to purchase land. Usually loans can be raised for the deposit, and the balance may be paid off in installments generated from farming profits.

Restrictions on the subdivision of farmland should also be

removed. Their effect is to prevent those who can afford only small units from becoming farmers. The theory behind restrictions is that the government should prevent the creation of nonviable units. But nonviable units would not survive if they were not propped up by various government policies designed to "keep white farmers on the land." There need be no concern about excessive subdivision. Given a free market system in which all farmers would stand or fall on merit, farmers on small portions that proved uneconomic would either sell them to others who would consolidate them, or lease them to farmers who would achieve economies of scale on many small portions owned nominally by others. In all countries with a successful agricultural sector and efficient land use, the trend has been for fewer and fewer of the population to farm and for each farmer to feed increasing numbers of people through increased productivity and efficiency.

Mineral Wealth

Nearly all of South Africa's mineral wealth—the diamond fields, gold fields, platinum mines, coal deposits, and iron mines—are concentrated in the northeast Cape, the southern and western Transvaal, parts of Bophuthatswana, and the northwest Free State. Together these areas make up less than 20 percent of South Africa's surface area. Is it fair that a few cantons should control all this wealth? We believe it is not unfair, and for a number of reasons. First, half the country's population is already concentrated in these areas. Second, the wealth of one district does not impoverish another. On the contrary, as long as there is free trade, the wealth of any part of the country benefits all other parts. This was demonstrated very clearly in the past when gold and diamonds were discovered and the entire country boomed.

Another point, perhaps the most important, is that mineral wealth plays a minor role in determining the prosperity of a society. As discussed in Chapter 4, many countries with abundant natural resources are poverty-stricken, whereas others with negligible resources are economic miracles. It is economic policy that determines whether countries, cantons, or communities prosper or starve.

To those who believe the mines should be nationalized, we point out that they already fall under the Mineral Rights and Mining Titles Acts. Mines are contracted out to the private sector through mining leases. The government gets its return from taxes on profits, volumes, wages, and salaries. This arrangement is more profitable for the government than running the mines itself; this would be true for any government. We advocate that mining policy be decided at canton level, and we would urge canton governments to privatize all minerals and apply the same regulations to mines as to any other business venture. Whatever policies are chosen, the optimal solution will soon become apparent.

If the architects of South Africa's future constitution decide that mineral wealth should remain under the control of central government so that profits can be redistributed, we suggest that this be done in the form of welfare vouchers or cash grants, which are the best means of ensuring that the money reaches the intended beneficiaries.

Welfare Vouchers

A number of goods and services in South Africa, such as bread, bus fares, housing, and education, are subsidized to help the poor. Most people assume that subsidies result in lower prices and do, in fact, help the needy. Unfortunately, they are mistaken. Subsidies actually increase prices. And instead of helping the poor, they benefit suppliers and manufacturers.

Studies show that subsidized bread is more expensive than unsubsidized bread currently being sold in the informal sector. This is in spite of the fact that informal sector bakers have to purchase their materials at retail prices, cannot advertise and distribute openly, and often have to pay bribes or fines.

Similarly, unsubsidized bus fares are cheaper than subsidized fares. In fact, the higher the subsidy, the higher the fares tend to be. When bus fares were investigated by the Free Market Foundation a few years ago, the most expensive bus fares in South Africa were those charged by white buses serving the richest suburbs of Johannesburg and Pretoria. They received the biggest subsidy— up to 65 percent. The cheapest bus fares were charged by the Indian bus operators in Durban, which were not only unsubsidized, but in some cases even paid taxes. Studies in America reveal a similar pattern.

The idea that subsidies actually increase prices is certainly surprising. How can it be explained? A clue to the answer lies in the fact that the most vociferous advocates of subsidies are the people who provide the product or service concerned. Bus operators spend hundreds of thousands of rands employing top public relations people to represent them in the media, to lobby the government, and to undertake research to establish a case for bus subsidies. The same is true of bakers who want bread subsidies or builders who want housing subsidies. If the true beneficiary were the consumer, it would be immaterial to the producer or supplier whether there were subsidies or not.

The reason so much time and money is spent in this way is that subsidies are in effect based on a percentage of production costs. For example, if the cost of a product or service is 10 million rands, the supplier might be subsidized by 10 percent, or 1 million rands. He is supposed to pass this on to the consumer in the form of lower prices. Clearly, his incentive is to maximize his cost: 10 percent of a high cost is more money than 10 percent of a low cost. Therefore, it is in the supplier's interest to maximize inefficiency and waste, to avoid innovation and risk-taking, to use accounting methods that overstate real cost, and to decrease productivity. Higher costs mean higher prices.

Not only do subsidies result in higher prices, but such benefits as do get passed on to consumers seldom reach the lowest income group. Millions of poor blacks in South Africa never buy bread in the formal sector, ride a subsidized bus or train, or live in a subsidized house. Their children do not get subsidized education. The people who benefit are the ones who paid the taxes with which the subsidies were financed in the first place—the middle and higher income groups.

Subsidizing manufacturers, distributors, suppliers, and administrators does not help the poor—it penalizes them. If the poor are to be helped they must be subsidized directly. The only way to do this is by giving them cash grants or welfare vouchers. Cash grants are preferable because each individual knows best what his own personal hierarchy of needs is. However, the fact that some might spend the money on gambling or liquor makes this an unpopular option. The alternative is welfare vouchers, which may be used by the recipient only for certain purposes. For example, poor people might be given transport vouchers, education vouchers, or food stamps. The vouchers must be freely usable in the marketplace.

Education

One of the great tragedies in South Africa today is the popular belief that the quality of education is a function of the quantity of money spent on it by government, and that therefore the problem of inadequate black education can be solved through free and compulsory state schools with the same per capita budget as white schools. On the contrary, evidence both here and abroad shows a correlation between increased state spending and declining education standards.

It is said that per capita spending on white education in South Africa is the highest in the world. Yet few would regard the quality of education as being anywhere near the top. In recent years there has been a disproportionate increase in education expenditure by government, averaging over 18 percent per annum. The 1984–85 budget proposed a 23 percent increase (R3.4 billion in one year). For blacks the budgeted increase was 26.3 percent. The amount budgeted for black education has increased by a staggering 2,648 percent since the 1972–73 financial year. These increases have not been matched by increases in quality, especially not in the view of discontented black school students, and a simple calculation shows that if the government were to spend the same on black, Coloured, and Indian students as it currently does on whites, it would soon be bankrupt.

There are several much more effective ways to improve the quality and availability of education. First, and most important, the government should encourage private education. Until recently it was doing just the opposite. Consider two examples:

During the 1960s, some concerned farmers in the Colesberg/ Norvals Pont area built a farm school at their own cost on Andries

Louw's farm. They arranged transportation to and from the school for the children of farm laborers, hired a teacher, and provided the necessary equipment and learning materials. The school was closed by Education Department inspectors. It did not comply with building or health regulations, it was not registered with the Education Department, it did not have an approved syllabus or the requisite number of pupils, and the teacher was not properly qualified. So black children who were getting reasonable and relevant education, however imperfect it may have been, at no cost or inconvenience to taxpayers or the state, were deprived of schooling. (This case, however, was different from countless others: the farmers fought back with the determination that distinguished their voortrekker ancestors. After a prolonged battle, in which even the Minister became involved, the school was allowed to reopen.)

The second example is a school owned and run by Mr. Monna in the Winterveld squatter settlement. There are no desks and the teachers are not "qualified." The children sit on long benches with their books on the floor. But three hundred children receive a basic education there at a cost to their parents of approximately R20 ($10) per year. Government inspectors have waged a long campaign against Mr. Monna, as they have against twenty or so other informal sector schools in Winterveld. Again, at no cost or inconvenience to the state or the taxpayer, these children who would otherwise be wholly uneducated are receiving some education. According to the headmaster, the children who go on to higher education from this primary school do better on average than those who have been to government schools.

Even if the state partially finances education, it need not provide it. Why not let the private sector provide schools while the government finances the students through education vouchers? Under a voucher system, each child of school-going age, regardless of race, would be entitled to an education voucher. These vouchers could be used at either private or government schools, and schools would compete with each other to attract students. Government schools need not be privatized, but neither should they be subsidized. They should compete on an equal basis with private schools.

A voucher system would encourage greater school autonomy

over curriculums and teaching methods. Education would be more relevant, and would cater to a kaleidoscope of different needs and preferences.

A voucher system would avoid the distortions created by subsidies. Vouchers could be of equal face value, or they could be graded according to the ability of the parents to pay for schooling. High income parents could supplement the vouchers to send their children to more expensive schools.

In addition to a voucher system, or as an alternative, there could be a tax-credit system. Parents who send their children to private schools would receive a tax credit in the form of an income-tax deduction. This would put an end to the present inequitable situation whereby parents pay twice for their children's education, once to the state and once to the private school. This in turn would encourage more people to use private schools. The credit could be limited to the per capita annual expenditure of state schools.

At present, childless adults and small families subsidize education for large families. The tax-credit system would also stop this from happening.

If all South Africans are to receive sufficient education at least to be numerate and literate, some government spending will have to be diverted from higher to lower education. The current extent of government spending on higher education favors people in the higher socioeconomic bracket at the expense of those in the lower bracket, since most people who pursue a higher education come from upper income groups. A voucher system would ensure that children receive the education they need and would automatically shift the emphasis to primary education, which is in greatest demand. Also, students who want to pursue higher education could be offered a government loan, to be repaid when they enter employment.

The devolution of control over schooling to canton and community government levels would go a long way toward solving the problem of race and education. Central government would no longer dictate whether schools should be segregated or multiracial; each canton would establish its own policy. Moreover, a canton could decide to devolve control even further, to local communities, municipalities, or school boards.

Privatization or a voucher system would ensure that schools provide what people want in terms of cost, quality, content, and racial mix. Schools that did not meet people's needs would go out of business. Private schools—with or without subsidies, vouchers, or tax-credits—would bring to education all the advantages of enterprise, motivation, innovation, and cost-effectiveness that flow from healthy competition.

Education has been a focal point of political unrest and boycotts because it is provided by central government. Decentralization and deregulation would not only improve the quality and quantity of education—they would depoliticize it.

Labor Relations and Trade Unions

In the system we have proposed, Article VII in the Bill of Rights entrenches freedom of association and disassociation. This includes the right of employees and employers to join or refrain from joining trade unions and employers' associations.

Trade unions would be free to organize nationally, cantonally, or within enterprises. Most of them would probably continue to operate much as they do now, subject to compliance with the Bill of Rights. Many would have a good chance of persuading one or more canton governments to adopt the policies they prefer. They would probably continue to operate through existing branches, and would deal with diversity in labor legislation in the same way as their counterparts in the many countries where labor laws are not uniform.

Some cantons might encourage different forms of labor organization, such as the enterprise unions found in Asia. There, unions are organized by company staff, so that instead of a boilermakers' union there would be, for example, a Barlow Rand Company union. Employees in enterprise unions see themselves as part of a team that includes managers and employers.

In some cantons government would not regulate labor at all, and labor relations would be subject to freedom of contract. Employers would decide whether or not to recognize unions, and nonparticipating employers and employees would not be bound by industrial agreements signed by others, as they are now. Disputes would be settled in civil courts under laws of contract.

The canton system allows all labor policies except those that contravene the Bill of Rights to be tried and tested. Employees, guided by labor activists, would seek employment only in cantons with satisfactory labor policies, and would flock to those that promoted their interests most successfully.

Privatization

The current South African government is already committed to privatization, and a high-powered Privatisation Committee has been appointed. Dr. Wim de Villiers, the prominent industrialist who recently conducted an investigation into the privatization of transport services, is now also a member of the Privatisation Committee. A committee is investigating the privatization of government forests, and a program for the privatization of most government low-income group housing has been devised. The government has announced a scheme for the progressive and genuine privatization of land in black areas. Private cable television has been authorized (albeit in the form of a monopoly granted to newspaper companies — a decision that defies comprehension). In some areas trash collection and other urban services have been privatized by local government. Various municipalities have organized a conference to explore practical strategies for privatization of their services. These are all big steps in the right direction, but it is very important that privatization be done in such a way as to avoid certain common pitfalls.

State monopolies must not become private monopolies. Privatization should occur only under conditions of free competition, and wherever possible it should be accomplished through public auction or open tender rather than private negotiation.

It should be implemented in a way that creates opportunities for small businesses, especially for blacks. For instance, if trash collection in KwaMashu is to be privatized, contracts should be offered for small areas to give small contractors a chance to compete for them. Similarly, park and road maintenance could be privatized so that individual contractors would be able to bid for the jobs. One large contractor may quote the best price on all contracts and get all or most of the work anyway, but at least the public will know that the best price has been obtained and that small business has been given a fair opportunity.

Although subcontracting is a popular way of transferring government monopolies to the private sector, there is no reason why most government enterprises should not be privatized completely. Virtually every function undertaken by government, especially local government, has been successfully privatized somewhere in the world. There are now private courts, police, water suppliers, and prisons.

A source of resistance to privatization is often the officials who believe their status and jobs are at risk. There is no need for this. Privatization can and should be implemented so as to offer new opportunities (such as a shareholding), greater job security, and higher incomes to existing employees who would then find themselves working for a private employer. There are many ways of achieving these objectives.

Whether or not a canton system is introduced in South Africa, the central government should divest itself of state corporations, parastatals, and state-protected monopolies through devolution, or better still, through privatization.

In a canton system, decisions regarding privatization would be in the hand of canton governments, and the demonstration effect would enable the public to see and experience for itself which approach is the most successful.

Urgent Reforms

There are a number of economic measures that the present government should undertake as a matter of utmost urgency in order to rapidly reduce political unrest and prepare for the successful introduction of a new order.

Racial Equivalence.   First and foremost, a Racial Equivalence Act should be passed that would sweep aside all laws governing blacks in black areas that differ from those governing whites in white areas. One of the major sources of frustration for blacks is the bureaucratic intervention and official discretion they face from day to day. No consultation is required in order to introduce equivalence, and white nationalists would not object because it would take place within existing black areas and homelands.

Inversion. At the same time, the principle of inversion should be introduced through a regulatory inversion act. At present the onus usually rests on people who want to enter the market to prove that in doing so they are not acting against the public interest. Instead, the onus should fall on anyone who opposes the opening of a business or the granting of a license to prove that such a move would be against the public interest. In other words, there would be a rebuttable presumption in favor of business people. This would make an enormous difference to the speed and facility with which people (blacks in particular) could enter business.

Small Business Deregulation. A Small Business Deregulation Act should be passed exempting all businesses employing fewer than twenty people from most or all regulations. This is by far the most effective way of encouraging small businesses. Such an act has been introduced in Ciskei with excellent results. During the first year of deregulation literally thousands of new small businesses sprang up throughout Ciskei—with no government subsidies to help them. Unemployment is falling. Consumers are getting better services and products at lower prices. Everyone is better off—except those who used to enjoy monopoly protection.

Free Enterprise Zones. In recent years, hundreds of free trade zones have been created around the world to encourage the development of new businesses and additional employment opportunities. Free enterprise zones are currently being developed in Natal (Zero Based Regulation Areas, or ZEBRA zones). Natal's example should be followed throughout the country.

The main objection to free trade zones is that by their nature they bring about economic and social distortion by causing an artificial movement of investment and people from one place to another. However, the advantages of free trade zones would far outweigh their disadvantages. They would give blacks a chance to enter and participate in the market economy before they are enfranchised. Free trade zones also create a demonstration effect. When the evils from which these regulations are supposed to protect us do not occur on a large scale, governments will be encouraged to extend deregulation to other areas of activity.

The Power to Expedite Urgent Reform

In President Botha's "Rubicon" speech on August 15, 1985, he said, "I am of the opinion that there are too many rules and regulations. . . . Even if I as State President have to take power during the next session of Parliament so as to enable me to deregulate in the interests of the country, I will do so!"

The Temporary Removal of Restrictions on Economic Activities Bill was passed in mid-1986, granting President Botha these powers. The government has lost a lot of its credibility because its inaction speaks louder than its words. Now it is essential that it move fast. We therefore advocate that the State President make use of his power to deregulate; to exempt any kind of enterprise from statutory law; to exempt defined areas (free zones) from specified measures, regardless of the size of businesses within those areas; and to repeal all laws that discriminate on the grounds of race. This is the only way to ensure that civil servants, some of whom may oppose change, will not, either deliberately or inadvertently, sabotage socioeconomic reform.

CHAPTER 16

The Legal System

Law is often but the tyrant's will, and always so when it violates the rights of an individual.

—Thomas Jefferson

A FREE SOCIETY IS CHARACTERIZED by the rule of law, an unfree society by the rule of man. To achieve true justice in South Africa we must reduce the rule of man and increase the rule of law.

Common Law

Over the centuries, common law systems have developed in societies throughout the world on the basis of what the "reasonable man" thinks is just or unjust. Despite certain differences, almost all systems of common law protect fundamental individual freedoms such as those we have listed in the proposed Bill of Rights, and prohibit basic violations of person and property such as theft, arson, fraud, assault, and murder. The application of common law varies from one society to another, even from one community to another, but the substance remains the same.

In South Africa common law is consistently and unambiguously embodied in the Roman-Dutch common law system.

Statutory Law

Statutory law is the body of laws built up through government legislation and regulations. The purpose of statutory law is to change or supplement the common law.

Discretionary Law

If laws, be they common laws or statutory laws, are applied according to clearly stated criteria, we have objective law. If, on the other hand, officials have the power to apply the law according to their own subjective views, then we have discretionary law, or the rule of men.

In Chapter 5 we showed that perhaps the greatest disadvantage experienced by blacks in South Africa is that they live in a world of discretionary law. They have no way of knowing, when they apply for a license or almost anything else, whether they will be successful, because their success does not depend on compliance with objective criteria, but on the whim of the officials in charge.

Discretionary law is bad law, and should have no part in any just legal system. For example, if a trader must be licensed and must comply with certain standards, the law should set forth the required standards unambiguously, so that any individual who complies with these requirements will be entitled to a license. There should be no application procedure whereby, in the name of the so-called public interest, administrative officials or boards may grant licenses to preferred people or refuse them to those who, for some reason, are out of favor.

All evidence regarding eligibility under various regulations should be given in public hearings, and written evidence should be freely available to the public. Deliberations of official bodies should be open to the public, and these bodies should be required to give reasons for all their decisions.

At present, countless official decisions, especially those regarding blacks, are made behind closed doors, and there is no accountability to the public.

Limiting Legislation

Justice in a free society is based mainly on common law. The judiciary is independent of the legislature and all individuals are equal before the law.

We have advocated a strictly limited central government because we believe this is the best way to avoid the submergence of common law rights under a deluge of legislation. We have suggested further that central government be allowed to enact or administer laws only in those areas of authority specifically delegated to it by the cantons.

Five main areas of administration that might be assigned to central government have been outlined. However, as the relationship between the cantons and central government would be essentially contractual, groups of cantons might choose to delegate further functions. For example, the coastal cantons might delegate control over the beaches. In any event, the more limited the functions of central government, the less likelihood there is that the common law will be overburdened.

The Importance of Independent Judiciaries

If a limited government constitution and bill of rights are to be effective, they must have the protection of an independent judiciary. In other words, the judiciary must be free from any influence or pressure by the government or any other lobby. True independence means much more than a mere policy declaration to that effect; the judiciary must be equal to the central executive and, like it, subject only to the constitution.

Since the judiciary is a branch of the government, true independence is problematic. However, a number of measures have been devised to protect judicial independence. One is security of tenure for judges: once a judge is appointed, he may not be dismissed — except under the most extreme conditions such as insanity or conviction of a serious crime — regardless of how offensive the government finds his judgments.

Another method is to leave the appointment of judicial officers largely in the hands of the legal fraternity. This is based on the assumption that the legal fraternity is incorruptible, which unfortunately is not necessarily so. In the United States, many public officials such as judges, attorneys-general, and police chiefs are elected by the citizens. This may be a better way of ensuring their independence.

In many western countries there is a popular view that the jury system guarantees judicial independence. However, there are serious problems with this. For example, jurors may be susceptible to the influence of popular and media opinion.

Some people argue that the judiciary will be truly independent only if courts are privately owned and run. Courts would compete with one another and litigants would agree to the jurisdiction of a court or group of courts that had established a reputation for being efficient, objective, and just. Once considered highly unorthodox, this idea is gaining popularity and there are now private courts in the United States. The increasingly popular system of arbitration in South Africa is similar to a private court system.

Some countries — the United Kingdom, for example — have a system of lay magistrates. Whereas South African magistrates are full-time civil servants, lay magistrates are respected citizens in the local community, such as school principals and doctors. They evaluate the evidence and determine the court's ruling with the aid of the clerk of the court, who advises them on questions of law.

There are interesting similarities between lay magistrates and the traditional courts of black chiefs and headmen in South Africa. Under the conditions of judicial devolution that we propose for the canton system, we would expect most of these different methods of administering the law and appointing officials to be used in various forms and combinations. The demonstration effect would help bring about the best judicial system.

Current South African Courts

There are currently three tiers of courts in South Africa. Magistrates' courts are the inferior courts and make up the lowest tier. They have limited jurisdiction and deal with petty infractions in civil and criminal cases. Black chiefs and headmen try cases that involve breaches of tribal common law (customary law) at this level, and the recently introduced small claims courts, which hear only civil actions, are also inferior courts.

Above the magistrates' courts are the supreme courts. There are supreme courts in each province, and they have unlimited jurisdiction. People whose cases have been tried in magistrates' courts have the right of appeal to supreme courts, and serious civil and criminal cases are automatically tried there.

Those who are not happy with the judgment of the supreme court have the right of appeal to the highest court in the country, the appeals court in Bloemfontein.

Canton Courts

We have recommended that South Africa be divided into cantons based on magisterial districts. Thus, while canton boundaries in their final form will not conform exactly to existing magisterial districts, it is likely that every canton will have an established magistrate's court within its area of authority. Courts at this level would vary a good deal from canton to canton in accordance with customary law (the common law of different cultural groups) and local administrative systems.

Supreme courts would also be controlled by canton governments. The existing infrastructure could be retained virtually as is, with existing supreme courts falling under the joint administration of surrounding cantons. Some cantons might prefer to establish their own second-tier court, as some homelands have done, but this should not interfere with the right of appeal to the appeals court. This would remain under central government control.

Recognition of Customary Law

A major advantage of a system of independent canton courts is a substantially increased respect for, and recognition of, customary law. When the judiciary is centrally controlled, the legal system of one group is inevitably imposed on others. This is a serious problem in a heterogeneous country. At present, South African law does recognize African customary law, but no formal account is taken of the differences between black tribes. Nor is the customary law of other groups such as Hindus and Moslems recognized.

Differences in customary law arise mainly in regard to "the law of persons," i.e., laws relating to matrimony, divorce, children, and inheritance. Given the dynamic nature of the canton system, it is likely that cantons with many Indian citizens would provide for differences between Indian and European law. Similarly, areas with substantial numbers of, say, Sothos or Xhosas would probably respect the customary law of those groups.

To ensure that customary law does not violate constitutionally entrenched individual rights, we propose that all people be free to elect the legal system of their choice. This already occurs to some extent in South Africa: the judge or magistrate may determine, at the request of the parties involved, whether Roman-Dutch law or tribal law applies in a particular case. In other parts of Africa too, there is a limited choice of different common law systems.

Some cantons might introduce the concept of class action. This, unfortunately, is alien to our current system but is being introduced in Ciskei. In the case of a class action or public interest action, an action can be brought to court against someone who is committing fraud or selling contaminated food. Public interest actions largely circumvent the need for health and safety legislation and all its attendant ill effects.

One of the greatest problems with our current judicial system is that law is effectively accessible only to the very poor, who qualify for legal aid, and to the well-to-do. It is likely that, with a variety of systems and with small claims courts and customary courts, access to law would become easier and cheaper.

Conflict of Laws

Clearly, if laws differ from one canton to the next, some of them will conflict. This is not a new problem. It occurs in Switzerland, the United States, and all other federal systems in which different constituent units have different laws. It also occurs between countries and to a limited extent between the provinces in South Africa.

We do not need to re-invent the wheel; an entire body of law has been built up over time to settle disputes resulting from conflicting laws. In cases regarding contracts, for instance, the law of the place in which a contract was concluded is usually invoked.

In some cases there may be conflict between cantons or communities. For example, some areas might want to control rabies through compulsory inoculations, while others might not. If such matters are not settled in the supreme court, they can be settled by the central government appeals court, which would act in the canton system the way an international court does in disputes between countries.

Legal Precedent

The practice of judicial precedent applies in South Africa: when there is a legal dispute the court settles the point by referring to previous judgments in similar cases. If a higher court has made a decision regarding a point of law, its decision is binding on all lower courts and virtually binding on equal courts throughout the country.

In the system we propose, appeals court decisions would be binding on every court in the country. This would ensure that individual rights are protected. However, each canton would be free to adopt its own policy on decisions made in the courts of other cantons. Some might pass a law to the effect that judgments made in other cantons would have the same force in their own courts. What is more likely is that groups of cantons, and conceivably all cantons, would enter into judicial treaties regarding such questions as legal precedent, reciprocal enforcement of judgments, and procedures for serving court documents across canton boundaries. These questions would probably be resolved in much the same way that they are now. Some cantons may adopt an entirely different legal system, but this seems highly unlikely.

Central Court of Appeal

To protect individual and canton rights laid down in the national constitution, we advocate an independent central court of appeal that would review the decisions of canton courts.

An independent court of appeal helps to avoid the possibility of local ethnic or cultural domination or miscarriage of justice. In any legal system it is essential to be able to take certain matters beyond local jurisdiction to a court in which there is some guarantee of an objective trial. All citizens would have an entrenched right of appeal, first to the highest court in the canton, then to the central court of appeal.

The court of appeal would apply the law of the canton in which the case originates. There is substantial precedent for this. Citizens of commonwealth countries, for example, have the right of appeal to the Privy Council in London.

The present South African appeals court in Bloemfontein handles appeals that must be judged according to laws that differ from province to province. It is also the ultimate court of appeal for three of the four independent homelands, which have increasingly dissimilar legal systems. (For instance, all four have repealed all racially discriminatory legislation and changed their tax rates, labor laws, and licensing laws. Two of them have a bill of rights.) The Bloemfontein appeals court is the ultimate court for cases based on both African customary law and Roman-Dutch common law.

If all the cantons are to have confidence in the central government judiciary, special care must be taken to ensure its independence. In addition to the precautions already proposed, there might be provisos to the effect that there may not be more than one judge from any one canton; that a certain number of cantons may veto the appointment of a judge; and that the state attorney be elected or nominated by cantonal rotation. Certain conventions would probably evolve, as they have done in the United States and Switzerland, to take account of ethnicity and socioeconomic factors. A recent U.S. Supreme Court judgment ruled that, unless ethnicity is taken into account in the selection of jurors, proceedings may be set aside. It found that a black accused of murder was entitled to insist on the inclusion of blacks in the jury.

South Africa's judiciary has a reputation, even among the current government's bitterest enemies, for a reasonable degree of courage and independence. The lower courts sometimes have been suspected of ethnic bias, but there have been many higher court judgments against the state on sensitive matters, especially in recent times. For example, in the Ngwavuma case, a government attempt to cede land to Swaziland was set aside. In the Komani and Rikoto cases, judgments were made against government policy regarding influx control. And recently, members of the UDF were released on bail against an order by the attorney-general. The government accepted the court rulings in all of these cases.

There is no perfect judicial system, but there is no reason why South Africa should not have a judicial system as good as the best in the world.

Conclusion

We propose that each canton choose its own legal system, and we have offered arguments in favor of an objective system based primarily on common law.

It is conceivable that some or many of the cantons would reject these ideas and that South Africa will end up with a majority of totalitarian states. But we think this is extremely unlikely. All available experience shows that when power is devolved societies tend to move toward greater personal freedom. As long as people are free to move, they will move to where freedom and justice can be found.

In a canton system, there would be competition between legal systems. Those that provided the most objective, equitable law would serve as models for the others.

CHAPTER 17

Strategy

Change does not roll in on the wheels of inevitability. It comes through the tireless efforts and hard work of those who are willing to take the risk of fighting for freedom, democracy, and human dignity.

—Allan Boesak, 1983

IN THE COURSE OF THIS book we have considered the political and economic realities and dynamics of contemporary South Africa, as well as some of the historical factors that produced them. We have described in detail a system we believe would meet the needs of all South Africans and achieve lasting peace, prosperity, and freedom.

We have discussed where we have come from and where we want to go. The question remains—how do we get there?

In answering this question, we will consider the current climate of opinion and whether it is conducive to radical change in the direction of greater individual freedom and responsibility; the steps the present government must take to generate maximal support for thorough reform; the specific means by which a change from the current system to a canton system would be implemented; and ways in which ordinary people can contribute.

Fertile Soil

Throughout the world there is a clearly detectable trend away from paternalism and statism towards individualism and personal responsibility. Since World War I, there has been a massive growth in government throughout the world. Now the pendulum is swinging the other way. The public rebellion against bureaucracy and excessive government interference manifests itself everywhere. De-nationalization and privatization are taking place not only in the United Kingdom and the United States, but also in communist countries. The socialist government in Italy is privatizing the telephone system. China is making significant free market reforms and even has some privately owned profit-making roads! India under Rajiv Gandhi is following suit. So is the Soviet Union under Mikhail Gorbachev.

The belief that the state can produce wealth and legislate equality is dying. Few academic economists today defend central planning. In a survey of American economists in 1978, about 85 percent agreed on basic free market propositions. This trend among economists, which is observable in South Africa as well, is part of a general swing back to free markets.

South Africans are ready for change. Even those who are not realize that it is inevitable nonetheless. But political groups in South Africa are notable for their inability to agree with one another. None represents anything approaching a majority of South Africans and none has come up with a plan that is attractive to all.

The strength of the solution outlined in this book lies in the fact that it offers an option that can meet the needs of all South Africans, except for the ultra left- and right-wing radicals who will oppose any peaceful resolution of our problems. South Africa is in such ferment that we believe our people can and will adjust to something new very quickly.

The Current Government's Role

The Nationalist government has an electoral mandate to bring about real reform. That is what it must do. President Botha has stated the government's objectives, which are to bring about genuine democracy, universal suffrage, and equality before the law within a system that will protect minority rights. The time has come for the government to take steps toward a system that embodies these objectives and to prove to South Africa and the world that apartheid is indeed "outdated."

Many political groups have called for a national convention where representatives of all South Africans can negotiate a solution. There are several difficulties with this idea, however, the greatest being the "Catch 22" regarding representation of blacks. Many black leaders are not prepared to negotiate until the government has spelled out a plan to dismantle apartheid — i.e., until the government has found a solution. At the same time they insist that a solution cannot be found without negotiation.

Even if black leaders could be persuaded to attend a national convention, it would be difficult to ascertain the real representatives of the people. So many organizations and parties claim to represent blacks that the total of alleged support for all these groups is equivalent to several times the total black population. Public opinion surveys are of little help, because they produce conflicting results that tend to reflect the ideological predispositions of the researchers (see Appendix II).

Another serious drawback of the national convention idea is that those groups that did attend almost certainly would be unable to reach agreement: differences between them run too deep. Rather than bringing together a group of people with axes to grind and ideological positions to defend, the government should decide on a workable solution and call for negotiation and discussion concerning the basic idea.

The purpose of the convention would be to develop a solution and to decide how power is to be shared. If the government decided to implement a canton system, half of the convention's task would be done. The question of power-sharing would become a nonissue, since central government in a canton system would be so limited that at the national level there would be little power to share.

The government should appoint experts to draw up a draft constitution and detailed proposals. Simultaneously it should employ a top public relations company, as it has done for the current reforms, to "sell" the solution both domestically and internationally. A diplomatic initiative should be launched to gain the support of as many foreign countries as possible. Foreign governments should be informed that South Africa is to have a multiparty democracy with universal franchise and no statutory discrimination. They should be asked, as a gesture of encouragement and goodwill, to terminate sanctions and boycotts and to stop supporting guerrilla movements. Apartheid is a cancer that can be destroyed in one of two ways. Either the patient can be clubbed to death, or the cancer can be removed through careful surgery and the patient nursed back to health.

To de-escalate political unrest and violence that threatens South Africa with a fatal civil war, the government should lift the state of emergency immediately and introduce racial equivalence, meaningful small business deregulation, free enterprise zones, and the principle of inversion, as discussed in Chapter 15. It is unlikely that any of the major political groups would object to these measures.

Next, all political prisoners—including Nelson Mandela— should be released, and all banning orders on people and organizations—including the ANC—should be lifted. Consultation and negotiation should take the form of informal contact with key people and the submission of evidence to the present Special Cabinet Committee on Constitutional Affairs, or to a specially appointed constitutional commission.

Numerous aspects of the model we have proposed must be considered and debated. Many of them, such as the sunset clause and the use of magisterial districts as a departure point, lend themselves to negotiation. These negotiations should start as soon as the government opts for the canton model.

There is no logical reason why the various political groups should reject a solution that fulfills their requirements simply because it is being implemented by the current government. Most parties are calling for the eradication of statutory discrimination, universal franchise, the recognition of minority rights, and genuine control by people over their own lives. If the government is openly committed to a plan that meets all these requirements, it should receive the support of all other groups.

When a draft constitution has been finalized to the government's satisfaction, the public should be given the opportunity to study and debate its contents thoroughly. It should then be put to a national referendum in which all adult South Africans would vote.

The Nationalist government was elected by whites and is answerable to them. This precludes a national multiracial election without their permission, but it does not preclude a national referendum. Some will argue that a new constitution should first be put to the white electorate. But it would be an important sign of good faith to begin the new era with the first genuine universal plebiscite in South Africa's history.

As a compromise, whites might vote on a separate roll, and the adoption of the constitution could be made conditional on receiving their support. However, we believe that if the canton system is properly understood, a majority of all ethnic groups will support it.

Implementation of a Canton System

Once cantonization has been accepted in principle, the Judicial Delimitation Commission would go into action. Delimitation Commission courts would sit in all the provinces simultaneously to receive evidence regarding canton boundaries. As there will not be enough judges to staff them, they should be supplemented by politically neutral black, Coloured, and Indian academics, school principals, professionals, and businessmen.

Maps showing the boundaries of magisterial districts should be printed in local papers. The courts would hear evidence as to whether these boundaries should become canton boundaries or should be altered. The delimitation courts would consider not only submitted evidence but would also undertake their own inquiries into local public opinion. There should be a presumption in favor of magisterial districts and the onus should fall on those who do not want the current magisterial district boundaries to prove that other boundaries would be better.

Once a canton boundary ruling has been made by the court it must be put to a referendum of all the people living in the area concerned. Delimitation decisions would be made with varying speed, depending on the actual agreement or dissension among residents of the area involved. If a court decision were rejected in a referendum, the court would have to go back to the drawing board.

From the time the courts start receiving evidence regarding the boundaries of a proposed canton, they would have two years to make a ruling. At the end of that period, failing a decision to the contrary, magisterial districts and subdistricts would automatically become cantons.

As soon as a canton's boundaries have been approved by the majority of its citizens, it should be issued a charter and granted full independence, subject to the condition that it hold an election within six months. When a canton government has been elected, it can decide whether to draw up a constitution for the canton.

Canton laws would be those of the present system until they are changed by the canton or community government. This is the normal procedure when devolution takes place. The administrative infrastructure would also remain until changed by the canton government.

Decentralization and Devolution

One of the few blessings of the homeland system and the constitutional changes that have occurred in South Africa in recent years is that we now probably have more experts on the mechanics of restructuring and decentralizing government than any other country in the world. The degree of devolution under the homelands system has varied from the transfer of four or five areas of concern to local government, to full independence in the national states. Each case has been different, and so it would be with cantonization.

During the decentralization process all existing local administrations would continue essentially as they are. Most administrative structures between them and central government would fall away, and the civil servants who head them would be elected locally and would hold office locally rather than in Pretoria or Cape Town. They would be the most senior officials at the local level and would be directly answerable to local politicians.

At least initially, in many cases local people would not have the expertise or experience required to assume high levels of responsibility. In such cases, officials in the central government structure could be seconded to local government, as was done during decolonization and again when the homelands were established. Areas that do not already have local administrative structures could continue to make use, for example, of the Regional Development Boards or Regional Services Councils, which they would then control. Cantons that so desired could subsequently form local boards or contract out local administrative functions to private enterprise.

Further devolution to local communities will be decided by canton governments and popular initiatives. Communities might be based on electoral wards, local authority areas, or taxpayers' associations.

In the period up to the chartering of cantons, unbanned political groups will have time to establish themselves and multiracial parties will be formed. All political groups will campaign, and probably will offer evidence to the Delimitation Courts regarding boundaries. Whites, blacks, Indians, and Coloureds in racially mixed magisterial districts will have time to negotiate with one another—what Beckett calls the "horsetrading of a marketplace democracy" will occur.

To show more precisely how devolution would occur, we will discuss an example—education—in greater depth.

An Example of Devolution: Education

Currently, apart from homeland education, all black education is administered by a central department, but every school has a parent-teacher committee and a governing body. The administration of white education is somewhat different and varies from province to province. In general there is a local school board in each magisterial district. For each school there is usually a school committee. In the Cape Province, for example, parents exercise a considerable degree of control. Transvaal school committees, in contrast, have very little say.

Above the school boards are regional inspectorates and provincial education departments. Above them is the Department of National Education, which has very little direct control.

Devolution would be initiated in white areas simply by severing the little control that central government presently has over the provinces. Next, each canton would take over its own existing school board or boards. Cantons without school boards could establish them. Provincial education department officials could be seconded to local levels either temporarily or permanently through a gradual process differing from canton to canton. Groups of cantons with compatible or shared interests might form Education Coordination Committees or Regional Education Councils. At present there is a network of multilateral and bilateral committees and working groups between the homelands and the Republic of South Africa. These could be phased out or continued, according to each canton's preference.

Within each canton control over education could be devolved further to local communities, as it is in the United States, Switzerland, West Germany, and Belgium. Control of education by local committees would ensure that schools meet the requirements of local parents and teachers.

Although each black school has its own governing body and parent-teacher committee, these organizations have almost no autonomy. They have no budget and no control over teachers or curriculum and are not permitted to make decisions even on issues unrelated to education policy.

A black school committee in the Transvaal, for example, recently decided that its school should be supplied with electric power. Committee members informed the Department of their intention, and when no objection was raised they collected R10 ($5) from the parents of every child to pay for electrification. On the day the electrician was to start work, they received an urgent memo from the Department forbidding them to make any changes to the school building pending a departmental investigation of the matter.

The frustration experienced by black school committees is immense. They are desperate for autonomy. All that needs to be done is to cut the links with the central department and let them run their own affairs. There are already committees for chairmen of school governing bodies; these could continue to liaise should they wish to do so.

In the course of cantonization, many black and white schools would fall into the same cantons. They could all be administered by a canton school board, or retain local autonomy and establish whatever connection with each other they wish. State-owned schools would have to be open to children of all races.

Some people think there should be a central governing body to set standards and approve the curriculum. South Africans have become accustomed to centralization and uniformity of standards. The notion that uniform educational standards are possible, however, is mistaken. Schools inevitably vary, both in the quality of their teachers and in the quality of the education they offer. When employers evaluate the qualifications of a job candidate, they assess his ability through interviews and tests. They also consider the reputation of the school or university he attended. This is true throughout the world: universities — and more specifically, particular faculties within universities — acquire international reputations for the excellence or inferiority of their graduates.

Currently AZAPO is instituting a system of private education as an alternative to government schools, and is soliciting recognition of its qualifications directly from the business community. One can safely predict that employers will be objective. All they are concerned about is the quality of the person they employ.

Cantons that adopt the voucher or tax credit system discussed in Chapter 15 will have the fewest problems with education, since under this system the standard of education will be left to market forces. Parents and students will pursue the best and most relevant education their vouchers can buy, and schools will compete for their patronage.

Conclusion

The existing government must make the necessary moves to see South Africa on the right course. It is much more likely to make those moves if there is a visible groundswell of support for a canton system among ordinary South Africans as well as in the international community.

Once the government has introduced the canton system, an evolutionary process will take over. Legal, economic, and social factors will change to reflect the new order. Unpopular institutions will disappear, and unacceptable laws will be repealed.

Competition between different political, economic, legal, and social policies will bring the best to the fore, and the involvement of all South Africans in all decisions affecting their own lives will bring prosperity and peace to this divided and unhappy land.

PART FOUR _____

The Future

> *Don't imagine that you will encounter*
> *a perfect world. . . . Here on earth*
> *there is no perfection: but the closest*
> *approach to perfection is the progress*
> *achieved by the continual striving for*
> *that unreachable perfection.*
>
> —Langenhoven

Part Four is an optimistic speculation on what the future may hold for South Africa. Although some names and places and a few details are drawn from reality, most of the events, attitudes, and characters are purely imaginary. But they are no less important for that.

EPILOGUE

The World
Within One Country

Imagine reading this cover story in the *International Tribune* of December 28, 1999:

On this, the eve of the twenty-first century, the media worldwide are focusing on the major developments of the last hundred years. Undoubtedly one of the greatest success stories of the century has been the transformation of South Africa from a conflict-ridden and divided country to one of the world's most stable and prosperous nations.

Many people have forgotten how insurmountable South Africa's problems seemed in the 1980s. Would there be a military coup? A full-scale violent revolution? Big power involvement? Few were optimistic despite President Botha's assurances that a peaceful solution would be found.

The new constitution was approved by a healthy majority in the first truly national multiracial referendum in December 1989. However, few were convinced that it could accommodate political policies that seemed wholly irreconcilable, or that it would achieve enduring peace. South Africans voted for it because it seemed the best of the various options open to them. Now South Africa is a model for the world, offering irrefutable proof that an extremely diverse society can prosper and thrive in peace and harmony.

Before we take a look at the four cantons that have attracted most international attention—Workers' Paradise, Witwaterberg (which may change its name to Blankeberg depending on the outcome of a canton referendum next week), Harrismith-QwaQwa, and Cisbo—we will briefly describe a few of the more conventional cantons.

During the two years following adoption of the new constitution, delimitation referendums resulted in a total of 108 cantons, with 27 part-cantons and 13 cantonettes forming over the next five years. Today there are a few unusual cantons and one or two rather strange communities, but the average canton is much like any other democratic country.

KwaNatal

After three years of shadow boxing, Zulu, white, and Indian moderates formed the Moderate Alliance Party, which surprised everyone by winning a landslide victory in the first election it contested. More government proposals have been accepted by the voters in referendums in KwaNatal than in any other canton.

KwaNatal has average tax rates, typical welfare programs, and basic civil liberties. The economy is fundamentally capitalist with social democratic elements such as modest consumer protection laws, state-owned utilities, trade licensing, and free and compulsory education. The official languages are Zulu and English. Buthelezi is still President and his following extends well beyond KwaNatal.

Apart from racial integration, the most conspicuous change has been the return of Durban's colorful rickshaws. "Just like the good old days," senior citizens say, recalling the time before the rickshaw clampdown in the 1950s, after which only a token number were allowed for tourists.

Along with rickshaw deregulation has come taxi deregulation. Now, just as in most other places in the world, KwaNatal's cities have an efficient taxi service. Indians play an important role in the canton's life. Because they are a minority in all but one area, special measures have been introduced to ensure that they have reasonable representation in government. There is also official recognition of customary Hindu and Moslem law for those who prefer it.

Consistent with worldwide trends, there have been steady but modest privatization, deregulation, and relaxation of censorship and liquor laws. "Zebras" (zero base regulation areas), which are Kwa-Natal's version of enterprise zones, are now common throughout the country.

Cape Flats Canton

Cape Flats canton is much like KwaNatal, except that the Presidency rotates for the time being between the two Reverends—Allan Hendrikse and Allan Boesak—and the official languages are Afrikaans, Xhosa, and English. Cape Flats is regarded as a low tax, low intervention area, and gambling has been authorized in two casinos.

The only observers who view Cape Flats with any real interest are political analysts. This is because, contrary to general expectations, the differences between Afrikaners and Cape Coloureds have evaporated, and the Reformed African National Congress–United Democratic Front (Cape) Party and the Labour Party work together in a way once thought inconceivable.

Apart from occasional reminders of the past, there is a prevailing atmosphere of normality. The most newsworthy events this year have been the disqualification of the first three runners in the Kuilsrivier Marathon and the burglary at Elseby's Pannekoek Paleis. Occasionally, demonstrations are organized by members of a radical Trotskyist movement, most of whom are Coloured students and factory workers.

Four Categories

The governments of most of the other cantons fall into one of four basic categories. Many are ruled by a moderate multiracial alliance, often including members of the old NP, NRP, PFP, Inkatha, UDF, and Sofasonke parties as well as members of the new Liberal and Reformed ANC (RANC) parties. The NP, Inkatha, and RANC are the only parties represented in all cantons.

In a second group of cantons, predominantly black parties or alliances have adopted socialist policies that have precluded any chance of a substantial nonblack following. Despite fears to the contrary, however, Indians, Coloureds, and whites in these cantons are adequately protected by the constitution.

In a surprisingly large number of cantons the major parties are no longer characterized by race. Most cantons have a two-party system, and candidates and officials are generally appointed on merit, regardless of race. As it happens, most politicians are black, many of the senior officials under them are white, and the balance of the civil service has much the same ethnic mix as the private sector.

There is also a fourth group of cantons with black nationalist governments. Until the sunset clause lapsed these governments practiced discrimination in favor of blacks. They still preach voluntary affirmative action, but most are beginning to moderate their policies as fewer and fewer blacks feel any need for special programs to assist them.

Now let us turn to the cantons that have been the subject of special interest and study among political scientists, sociologists, economists, and jurists — not to mention the general public — around the world.

These cantons have shown South Africa and the world that one country can contain political, economic, and social systems that differ from one another in almost every respect.

Workers' Paradise

Workers' Paradise canton is situated on the Vaal Triangle and has a population of about one million. Soon after chartering, the Marxist Alliance came to power. This was a coalition of the largely black AZAPO Youth Party, the Coloured Trotsky Party, Die Radikale Werkersparty (mostly Afrikaner unskilled and semi-skilled laborers), and the Communist Party (a small multiracial party led by academics). Even though these parties participated in what they denounced as "the system," the Security Police revealed that some of them had connections with the external wing of the Pan African Congress, which continued fighting for a few years because it maintained that the new constitution and Bill of Rights entrenched "bourgeois values."

The Marxist Alliance soon discovered that the only constraints it faced were the entrenched freedom of movement and property rights clauses in the Bill of Rights. These prevented the Alliance from freely expropriating land and businesses, and it was not able to create a "Haak en Steek Curtain," which some members would have liked. Also, because South Africa is a common customs and monetary area, the Alliance could not prevent people from taking their assets and leaving. Some people did leave, but many others, especially members of the emergent radical union movement, relocated there.

The Marxist Alliance lost no time in introducing pure communism. Surprisingly, this proved easier for the Alliance than for its counterparts in the Eastern Bloc, who have the COMECON customs union to contend with and are hamstrung by a conservative old guard that will not give real freedom to worker co-operatives and communes.

Sweeping reforms stunned observers. The canton adopted the name "Workers' Paradise," and the main towns became Maoville and Machelstad. Many black citizens donated their redistribution compensation checks to a government fund; this money was added to revenue gained from heavy taxes and used to buy out all private enterprises. Factories were handed over to worker co-operatives and farms were communalized. Civil servants took over the shops. Advertisements, billboards, and neon signs were ripped down, and all publications other than those issued or approved by the party propaganda office were banned.

When the Alliance was formed some hard bargains had to be driven. At the insistence of AZAPO Youth and the Radikale Werkers, there had to be some segregated facilities, such as public toilets, because they refused to mix with each other socially. Since the constitution specifies that governments must be colorblind, the problem was solved by turning segregated facilities over to the Public Workers Co-operative, which is controlled by COWPU, (Council of Workers' Paradise Unions), to which all unions must affiliate.

Critics have attacked such vestiges of apartheid in a Marxist canton. "This is quite different," a spokesman for the Quality of Equality Commissar explained. "This is a 'people's policy.' It is not imposed by white fascists. As far back as the early 1980s many of us in AZAPO and COSAS would have nothing to do with whites."

The government of Workers' Paradise has found that the canton system offers a unique benefit: there are no dissidents, counter-revolutionaries, or reactionaries. They have all left. That is why Workers' Paradise has become what it claims it is: the purest example of communism in the world.

The canton boasts of a completely egalitarian wealth distribution. The President never fails to mention that there is no unemployment, that class has been eliminated, and that nowhere else are workers so thoroughly in control of their own destiny.

Encouraged by this, most of the revolutionary socialists who had left South Africa have returned. Only two small extremist groups continue to cause trouble from time to time: the all-white army — the Herstigte Blanke Weermag (HBW) — which wants the restoration of classical Verwoerdian apartheid throughout South Africa, and Black Mamba, a regrouping of black guerilla movements that decided to carry on fighting for an unconditional handover of all of South Africa and SWA/Namibia.

Perhaps the most remarkable thing about Workers' Paradise is that the state is showing signs of "withering away," since devolution of power to workers *in situ* has been accompanied by a reduction of civil servants employed directly by the canton government.

The canton is the subject of interminable debate among academics. Critics point to low growth, the underground economy, and corruption. Others ask, what does it matter? Everyone is happy and no one has to live there. In fact the National Happiness Index (NHI) for the whole of South Africa, compiled by the Quality of Life Research Council (Qualrec) is at an all-time high and rising in Workers' Paradise.

Witwaterberg

Predictably, the process of reform produced a radical white racist reaction: the HBW military wing. In the late 1980s it had about one million followers, half of whom wanted to live in a white supremacist canton. The remainder were willing to live in multiracial conservative cantons with strict censorship, Christian national schools, and private whites-only clubs and social amenities. All of them contributed generously to the Wit Volk Fonds (WVF), a nationwide body that raised funds to finance segregated facilities. One of its major projects was to buy all the land in certain cantons and then to use private property rights to exclude blacks. Everyone was surprised to see how many blacks contributed to the WVF.

Witwaterberg is South Africa's notorious radical white separatist canton. When the new constitution was introduced, Witwaterberg had a small black majority, but the WVF undertook a successful campaign to persuade most white employers and landowners to replace many of their black employees with whites and to increase mechanization.

Farmers bought mechanized milking machines. Fast food outlets introduced disposable utensils so that they no longer needed a black staff to wash dishes. Manufacturers replaced many black laborers with machines operated by highly skilled white workers. White bus drivers and cash register operators were employed. Black tenants, such as attorney Gabriel Makopondo, who had become an accepted member of the local fraternity, were given notice on their leases. All leases in the black "lokasie" were terminated.

One of the most controversial developments in Witwaterberg was the mass dismissal of black workers. Most households had a black gardener and a maid who lived, often with their families, in servants' quarters adjoining their employers' houses. After considerable social pressure all domestics were laid off.

This measure sparked a curious debate in labor circles. The Domestic Employees' Rights Association (DERA), with the active support of the emergent union movement, had been a vociferous campaigner against the "exploitation" of domestic workers since the early 1980s. Many abuses had been exposed by its dedicated President, Ethel van der Merwitz. DERA stood for a national minimum wage and improved working conditions. No one was opposed to the idea of higher wages and good conditions, but some people argued that they might increase unemployment and thought that a low wage was better than no wage.

Prior to the layoff of black workers in Witwaterberg, Ms. Van der Merwitz exposed Witwaterberg whites on national TV as archetypal bigots, exploiters, and racists. Black workers there had the worst working conditions, the poorest housing, and the lowest wages. She cited one family that paid its maid only R40 ($20) a month, an amount that she showed was less than the family spent on one meal at Graaf's Boere Brunch every Thursday on the maid's night off. When the Witwaterberg layoff campaign began, DERA's Council was irreparably split. The black layoff campaign was succeeding, and might spread to other areas. Thousands of blacks could lose their jobs. How should DERA react? Should it call for all these blacks to be kept on under the intolerable working conditions it had condemned? Should it demand that black employees not only be kept on but also paid much more?

Witwaterberg's President, Mr. Staal Noordhuis, announced triumphantly that Witwaterberg would "no longer exploit blacks."

Witwaterberg, unlike the few other white majority cantons, had no desire to reach an accommodation with its nonwhite inhabitants. "The Bible is clear," insisted President Noordhuis. "We were created differently for a reason. Whites were destined to be the custodians of blacks, just as parents are of children, and blacks are to be the drawers of water and hewers of wood." He was stoically self-righteous in the face of lampooning and criticism, and became a folk hero in his little canton, which claimed to be the only place ever to achieve true apartheid.

By December 1997, when the sunset clause in the constitution lapsed, all the public and private facilities, all the land, all the houses in Witwaterberg were owned by whites. Now the only blacks to be found in the canton are daily commuters who are prepared to put up with racism because they are so highly paid.

The blacks who were laid off soon found jobs in the rapidly expanding industrial sectors of other cantons.

Servants' quarters have become garden flats for whites who moved into Witwaterberg. The old black locations have been converted into quaint "Chelsified" white lower-income areas.

Occasionally, even to this day there are unpleasant incidents, such as when "Bullfight" Nokokosi, as he was known to his friends, insisted on being served at Graaf's Boere Brunch. Or when President Noordhuis's nephew, nicknamed "Donderstorm" in recognition of his fearsome tactics on the rugby field, took after his gardener with a sjambok for pulling out his treasured waterblommetjies instead of khakibos weeds.

But most of Witwaterberg's critics concede that it has become a peaceful, quite harmless canton with a rustic character all its own. The few unfortunate incidents that occur are newsworthy only because they take place in Witwaterberg. One sociologist has observed that there are far fewer racial incidents in Witwaterberg than in Washington, D.C.

Harrismith–QwaQwa (H-Q)

No one could have predicted the incredible events that unfolded in Harrismith-QwaQwa, culminating in a happy ending with a unique twist.

In H-Q blacks outnumber whites by ten to one. Most blacks live in the area that used to be the Basotho-QwaQwa homeland in the southeast corner of the old Free State province, where H-Q borders on Lesotho and KwaNatal.

After delimitation, Paramount Chief Mopedi was elected canton President in a landslide victory. White and black radical candidates were routed; support for traditional chiefs was much more widespread than modernists had bargained for.

Black radicals were enraged, and a mood of despair descended on white nationalists. Farmers started neglecting their fields, businesses were put up for sale, and property values plummeted. "Women wept quietly in the kitchens and men worked silently in the fields; Parliament was in session and they feared that no man's property was safe." Township unrest increased.

But Chief Mopedi had no malicious ambitions. He wanted no more than official recognition of his tribal laws and customs and freedom and independence for all blacks.

Even though his people had suffered centuries of discrimination, he harbored no desire for revenge. The first thing Chief Mopedi did after becoming President was to call a canton convention at his tribal headquarters. His charisma and statesmanlike qualities were admired by onlookers everywhere. At the convention he announced his new policy of "parallelism," and explained that there would be no interference by his government with the local affairs of whites or urban blacks. The erstwhile QwaQwa homeland would become the QwaQwa tribal cantonette in which tribal law would apply.

In the black townships each person could choose whether to fall under the tribal system or the European system. In white areas there would be no "Africanization" policy. Whites who wanted separate private facilities would not be discouraged, nor would blacks be deprived of their blacks-only football league.

The political system he introduced was similar in many respects to that which had operated in the tricameral parliamentary system between 1985 and cantonization. In his own party, Chief Mopedi appointed a White Affairs Subcommittee, whose main task was to ensure that the whites' traditional way of life would not be unduly disturbed under black rule. Almost overnight property values soared above their pre-referendum levels. Harrismith-QwaQwa is now booming again. One filling station still has segregated toilets, and the Harrismith Jukskei Club admits only whites. No "colonial era" names have been changed, except that the canton has come to be known as "H-Q."

Cisbo

The last of South Africa's four most unusual cantons, the free market Ciskei-Border canton, now called Cisbo, has become a *cause célèbre* worldwide. During his Ciskei independence speech in 1981, President Sebe, now retired, announced that Ciskei was to become the "Hong Kong of Africa." He sometimes referred to Ciskei as the "Switzerland of Africa in the making." He could not then have had any idea that Ciskei and the Border Region would one day combine to form a canton much like those in Switzerland. On the contrary, independence was working so well for Ciskei that Sebe's government steadfastly resisted all efforts to reincorporate during cantonization.

Between 1984 and 1987, Ciskei's free market reforms were introduced in earnest. They included sweeping deregulation, the privatization of tribal land, and low taxes. That encouraged the establishment of many new businesses and industries. By 1990 Ciskei was booming. A respected American business journal called it "Africa's first economic miracle"— a far cry indeed from the gloom and doom depicted in the celebrated 1980 BBC documentary *Last Grave at Dimbaza.*

Meanwhile, whites in the Border Region (between Ciskei and Transkei) had lobbied since the late 1970s to become a free trade zone or a co-prosperity zone authority (COZA), and became known as the COZA (pronounced "Xhosa") group of cantons. They had learned much from their close proximity to Ciskei, and adopted similar laissez-faire policies. The serious "black spot problem" they had experienced before cantonization was solved automatically when blacks in those settlements obtained freedom of movement and freehold title and the right to go into business.

Inevitably, there were moves for a closer alliance with Ciskei. However, Ciskei was still an independent country, although not recognized by the United Nations. Since the cantons had no power to conduct foreign affairs, it was unconstitutional for the COZA cantons to negotiate with Ciskei. This led to a series of court actions and top-level debates called the Frontier Cases.

Most cantons, having black governments committed to the eradication of all vestiges of apartheid, wanted to force Ciskei to reincorporate. The COZA cantons tried to secede but could not get a sufficient majority in the referendum.

Time passed and emotions subsided. Then, when it was satisfied that it had nothing to lose, Ciskei proposed formal amalgamation with South Africa, subject to the creation of one large canton, the Cisbo canton, covering the entire area between the Great Fish River and Transkei.

At the formal signing ceremony President Sebe announced his retirement. He said that he had always advocated the restoration of his people's traditional territory to them and that he had always wanted a confederation of states, which was what the new arrangement amounted to. He had fulfilled his dreams of freedom, independence, democracy, and equality for his people, as well as high growth, development, and enduring peace.

Cisbo flourished and became a free market mecca. Not only did its economy become the freest on earth, but other radical deregulations occurred. As in some American states and Swiss cantons, *dagga* (marijuana), pornography, prostitution, and homosexuality were decriminalized. The coastal resort of Pleasure Bay grew into a mini-Monaco, with over twenty independent casinos, two privately owned deep-sea yacht basins, and several film production houses. It boasts deep-sea fishing, parachuting, water skiing, oriental pleasure palaces, countless "extravaganzas," stuntmen, boxing championships, golf, and much more. An incredible 50,000 new jobs have been created there alone. Cisbo's Pleasure Bay is now the world's most popular playground.

As always, success attracts criticism. Conservatives and socialists alike charge that Cisbo is causing unemployment elsewhere by attracting a disproportionate amount of investment. They have also accused it of moral decadence. On this issue several otherwise irreconcilable groups are united. Cisbo's numbered bank accounts are suspected of being a haven for laundered money.

The World Within One Country

It bears repeating that Workers' Paradise, Witwaterberg, H-Q, and Cisbo are so atypical that there is constant talk of threatening them with expulsion. Many people feel that there is a point at which a canton becomes so deviant as to be intolerable. There is growing support within Cisbo for secession, on the grounds that membership in the South African customs and monetary area is inconsistent with its otherwise laissez-faire policy. Even so, at the time of this writing, we are pleased to say that this is still just talk. There will never be a time when everyone is satisfied.

What is certain, though, is that "South Africa's problems," as they used to be called around the world, have been solved. All sanctions were lifted by 1990. South African athletes won 13 gold medals at the 1996 Lusaka Olympics. And Mandela, Botha, Van Zyl Slabbert, Buthelezi, Treurnicht, Tambo, Motlana, and Terre' Blanche have all become Presidents — of their own cantons.

Perhaps the last word should go to United Nations Secretary-General Artofon Glalkis. When he reported to the General Assembly after his second fact-finding mission to South Africa last April, he made this historic statement:

> The mistake we all made was to believe that a single political system would solve South Africa's problems. But the solution proved to be many different systems working simultaneously. We thought there should be one popular leader, but now there are many popular leaders working side by side.
>
> We thought a demagogue would preside over central government. Now a relatively unknown person does so. We demanded "one person, one vote" in a unitary state. South Africa chose "one person, many votes" in a cantonized state.
>
> We wanted single citizenship for all South Africans. Now they each have three citizenships—of their country, their canton, and their community.
>
> My predecessor said it took us too long to suspend South Africa from the General Assembly. I say it has taken us too long to readmit her.
>
> With her newfound diversity added to her heterogeneity, resources, beauty, and history, South Africa has truly become "the world within one country."

APPENDIX I

Bill of Rights

WE HAVE RECOMMENDED a canton system with a limited government constitution as the political solution for South Africa.

In the preceding chapters we have discussed various provisions that should be included in the constitution, notably a bill of rights. The Bill of Rights we propose would be an entrenched provision listing certain fundamental and inviolable rights of citizens and cantons. Amendments would require unanimous agreement by all canton governments and an 80 percent majority of voters in a compulsory national referendum.

We have suggested that a sunset clause might be included in the constitution: should some cantons not want to abolish discriminatory legislation immediately, they would be entitled to a twilight period of ten years in which to phase it out. This clause would override Articles I, III, V, VI(iii), VII, and X of the Bill of Rights until the sunset date, after which every canton would have to comply with all articles. Since most cantons would have a black majority, it is unlikely that more than a handful of them would make use of the sunset clause.

The Bill of Rights outlined here is written in lay rather than legal language. A definitive Bill of Rights would of course be carefully worded by legal experts.

Explanatory notes for each clause designated by an asterisk follow the text of the Bill of Rights.

BILL OF RIGHTS

PERSONAL RIGHTS

Article I   Equality

No law, practice, or policy of government at any level shall discriminate on the grounds of race, ethnicity, color, creed, gender, or religion, except that all existing discriminatory laws, practices, or policies shall continue until relaxed or repealed, or until the Sunset Date, whichever is the earlier.

Article II   Citizenship*

All people will be South African citizens who presently qualify for South African citizenship under the terms of the Citizenship Act, including those who did so prior to homeland independence, and those who would have qualified had the homelands not become independent. Every citizen is entitled to the citizenship of the canton and community of his or her birth, or of his or her permanent residence at the time of delimitation.

Article III   Universal Franchise

Every person of voting age shall be entitled to vote in all national referendums (and elections, if any) and in all elections and referendums of the canton and community of which he or she is a citizen.

Article IV   Referendums*

(i)   **Popular initiatives**
      Every citizen will have the right to launch a popular initiative calling for a referendum on any law, practice, or policy, or calling for a general election, subject to the following conditions:
      — at the national level, there being a petition by not fewer than 100,000 citizens entitled to vote;
      — at the canton level, there being a petition by 100,000 or 20 percent of the citizens of that canton entitled to vote, whichever is the lesser;

— at the community level, there being a petition by 50,000 or 20 percent of the citizens of that community entitled to vote, whichever is the lesser.

(ii)   Compulsory referendums
— Changes to ordinary provisions in the Constitution require the approval of a majority of the electorate in a national referendum. Changes to entrenched provisions require the approval of an 80 percent majority of the electorate in a national referendum.
— No canton boundary may be changed, including splitting from or amalgamating with another canton, unless approved by a majority of all the registered voters directly affected thereby. If a part of a canton wishes to split from an existing canton, the citizens in the remainder shall not have a vote in the referendum. But if that part is to amalgamate with or be incorporated into another canton, all the citizens of the latter shall be entitled to vote in a separate referendum.

Article V   Freedom of Movement

All citizens of South Africa may move freely from, into, or through all parts of the country upon public thoroughfares and in public places.

Article VI   Property Rights

(i)   Basic property rights*
All citizens of South Africa may own, acquire, use, and dispose of movable and immovable property.

(ii)   Expropriation*
It shall be unlawful for government at any level to confiscate, commandeer, or expropriate any private property (movable or immovable) except for bona fide infrastructural purposes: for national defense and security, where there is no reasonable alternative under due process of law, or for the purpose of settling a binding debt to the state.

(iii) **Right of Admission***

The proprietor or lawful possessor of any movable or immovable property may exclude or refuse admission to any other person.

(iv) **Nominative Boundaries***

Any landowner or group of landowners whose land is on a boundary between cantons may opt at any time for the boundary to be adjusted so as to place such land under the jurisdiction of a neighboring canton, subject to the agreement of that canton.

Article VII   Freedom of Association and Disassociation*

Any person may associate or transact with any other person or refuse to associate or transact with any other person for any reason.

Article VIII   Civil Liberties

There shall be freedom of speech and freedom of the press, subject only to considerations of public decency and safety according to the norms of the canton or community concerned.

Article IX   The Right to Trial and Due Process*

No person shall be convicted, sentenced, or imprisoned without due process of law, including the right to trial and habeas corpus, and there shall be no detention without trial.

Article X   The Right of Appeal

In respect of every judgment of the highest court in a canton or group of cantons, there shall be a right of appeal to the ultimate court of appeal, except that in a civil action parties may agree in advance that there should be no right of appeal.

Article XI   Minority Victimization*

Every minority group of people shall be protected from victimization by government at any level. What constitutes a "minority" or "victimization" shall be determined by the court according to the circumstances of each case.

Article XII Intimidation*

Every person and every group of people shall be protected from politically motivated intimidation by any other person or group, and upon conviction on an intimidation charge the court may impose the severest penalty permitted by law. In any event, the accused shall be sentenced to a term of imprisonment without the option of a fine.

CANTON RIGHTS

Article XIII   People's Congress

Every canton or part-canton shall be entitled to proportional representation in the People's Congress based on the number of registered voters in it.

Article XIV   Delegates' Congress*

All cantons shall be entitled to representation by an equal number of delegates in the Delegates' Congress regardless of their size or population, and all semi-cantons shall be entitled to be represented by half that many delegates.

Article XV   Canton Veto

Each canton has the right to veto any proposed amendent of any entrenched clause in the constitution and any proposed delegation of any power or function to the central government not already conferred by the Constitution.

Article XVI   Secession

Every canton has the right to secede from the country upon a declaration of secession being approved by not less than 80 percent of its registered voters, whereupon it shall become a sovereign independent state in accordance with international law.

Article XVII   Boundary Changes

Every canton and every part of a canton may, by referendum, as provided in the Constitution, break away from or amalgamate with any other canton.

Article XVIII   Constitutions and Bills of Rights*

Every canton may adopt its own constitution or bill of rights entrenched in such manner as the canton may determine, provided that any additional rights conferred upon its inhabitants do not conflict with the national Constitution.

Article XIX   Alliances

All cantons or communities are free to enter into alliances, agreements, or arrangements to their own satisfaction with other cantons or communities.

Article XX   Citizenship

Every canton may adopt its own citizenship policy subject to Article II, provided that no canton may grant citizenship to someone who is not a citizen of South Africa.

EXPLANATORY NOTES

II Citizenship

South African citizens would have to choose citizenship of either the canton of their birth or the canton of their permanent residence at the time of initial delimitation. The cantons may not refuse them, or strip them of citizenship for which they qualify at that time. After initial delimitation, canton governments may stipulate citizenship requirements for future citizens. Canton governments may offer to buy citizenship rights back from citizens who qualified at the time of initial delimitation.

IV Referendums

Universal suffrage is no guarantee that all laws introduced by elected representatives are supported by the majority. By granting citizens the right to call for referendums and ensuring that changes to the constitution are subject to referendums, the Bill of Rights helps guarantee basic democratic rights.

It is difficult to get 50,000 or 100,000 signatures on a petition, so the right to launch popular initiatives would not result in an excessive number of referendums, as some people fear. Also, Swiss experience shows that the administrative cost of referendums is very low. We suggest that this be contracted out to private enterprise.

VI (i) Basic Property Rights

In its literal sense, this clause would make all government intervention unconstitutional. This is not our intention. The clause is intended to protect every citizen's fundamental property rights according to reasonable definition, and in a final bill of rights the wording would need to be carefully worked out by legal experts.

VI (ii) Expropriation

Many of the worst injustices in South African history have resulted from the expropriation of private land by government. We have shown how the land rights of blacks were progressively eroded so that today they scarcely exist at all. We have discussed the extent to which Coloureds, Indians, and whites have also suffered loss of land, homes, and businesses as a result of expropriations by government.

To ensure that these injustices never recur, we propose this unambiguous anti-expropriation clause. This would prevent expropriation for other than "genuine" purposes, and in such cases proper compensation based on market value, sentimental value, and subsequent losses would have to be made.

If government at any level wanted land or other assets for any other reason, such as the provision of schools, housing, parks, or whatever, it would have to buy it by voluntary agreement just as anyone else would have to.

VI (iii)   Right of Admission

In South Africa, proprietary discretion has been violated by various acts, particularly the Separate Amenities Act, which dictate with whom people may or may not transact on their own property. In the United States and other countries, various measures dictate whom people must serve on their own property. By entrenching right of admission, South Africa would become the first country in the world with properly protected property rights.

VI (iv)   Nominative Boundaries

This novel clause is proposed so that landowners on boundaries between cantons will be free to nominate which canton they wish to join. Unpopular governments would lose citizens to neighboring cantons and find their boundaries closing in on them if they didn't change their ways.

VII   Freedom of Association and Disassociation

The right of people to mix with or separate from others as they choose is fundamental to a free society. Apartheid laws interfere with the right to associate; affirmative action laws with the right to disassociate.

This clause ensures that any individual or group of individuals acting in a private and voluntary capacity may discriminate in favor of or against any other person or group of people on the grounds of race, gender, religion, or otherwise for any reason and in any manner that does not entail a transgression of common law rights. This includes the right of companies to determine their own employment policies, and the right of private schools, clubs, and other organizations to refuse or admit members as they choose.

IX   The Right to Trial and Due Process

Although we do not condone it, if South Africans decide that there is to be detention without trial, it should be subject to authorization by a supreme court judge. Authorization would be granted only if there is evidence beyond a reasonable doubt that such detention is necessary for the safety of the state. In any such case, the following conditions should be met:

— The detainee must be maintained at all times in comfortable "civilian conditions."
— The detainee must have liberal access to friends, relatives, physicians, and legal counsel.
— Such detention should not exceed three months, except that detention for further periods of three months may be ordered upon the case for detention being re-established *de novo*.
— The detainee should retain all rights that are not in conflict with the basic objective of detention, including unlimited access to materials and literature.

XI Minority Victimization

Most white South Africans, and many Coloureds and Indians, fear that with universal suffrage the black majority will impose a system that does not recognize minority interests or that aims specifically to plunder nonblack wealth.

The principle has long been established in company law that victimized minorities have protection. We advocate that this be entrenched in the Bill of Rights so that any minority will be free to bring a court action to show that a given government measure, at any level of government, amounts to the abuse of majority power to victimize the minority.

XII Intimidation

Many people are afraid that, although the majority of South Africans are moderate and reasonable, when elections are held many may be intimidated by a handful of radicals into staying away from the polls or voting for political groups they would otherwise not support.

In order to discourage intimidation, we propose that it be a serious offense. In a final bill of rights, "intimidation" would need to be very carefully defined.

XIV   Delegates' Congress

Further subdivisions of cantons (cantonettes) will not be entitled
to representation in the Delegates' Congress.

XVIII   Constitutions and Bills of Rights

Here are examples of the additional rights cantons might introduce
in their constitutions. This list is not exhaustive, and some of these
rights are mutually exclusive:

- **Freedom of Contract:** the right to conclude any mutually voli-
tional agreement among any consenting adults whether commercial or social;
- **The Right to Work:** the right of anyone to obtain employment,
regardless of occupational licensing, minimum wage, or closed-
shop union provisions;
- **Conditions of Employment:** the right to minimum conditions
of employment such as annual leave, pregnancy leave, rate for
the job, occupational safety, etc;
- **Welfare Rights:** the right to a pension, unemployment benefits,
medical aid, etc;
- **Freedom of Speech and Press:** i.e., going further than the central government bill of rights, under which cantons or communities could impose restrictions in regard to public safety or
indecency;
- **Academic Freedom:** the right of educational institutions to
determine their own admission criteria, course content, staff
appointments, student rights, etc.
- **Property Rights:** i.e., the protection of property rights beyond
that provided in the central government bill of rights.

APPENDIX II

Opinion Surveys

Schlemmer's Findings

IN 1984 LAWRENCE SCHLEMMER of the Centre for Applied Social Sciences at the University of Natal conducted research into "black industrial worker attitudes" towards political options, capitalism, and investment.

His research team interviewed 551 black production workers ranging from 16 to 50+ years old in Johannesburg, Durban-Pinetown, Port Elizabeth, East Rand, West Rand, Pretoria, and the Vaal Triangle. Some 65 percent were lower semi-skilled and unskilled and 35 percent were higher semi-skilled and skilled.

His question was:

"Here is a list of organizations. Which one of these organizations do people like yourself support most? Which other one do people like you support?"

The results were:

	Witwatersrand and Port Elizabeth	Durban
	1st Choice %	1st Choice %
ANC/Nelson Mandela	27	11
UDF	11	23
AZASO	1	1
AZAPO	5	1
Inkatha/Buthelezi	14	54
Sofasonke	15	6
Other—diverse	5	4
None	22	—

If these results are regrouped according to how radical the groups represented are, the following picture emerges:

	W/PE %	Durban %
Moderate(Ink/But/Sof/none/other)	56	64
Fairly radical (ANC/Mandela/UDF)	38	34
Radical (AZASO/AZAPO)	6	2

We have included "none" and "other" as moderate because most "other" groups and community leaders are moderate. Schlemmer assumes that there is no "none" in Durban because they are absorbed into Inkatha, and that their counterparts elsewhere are probably moderates in a political vacuum.

The "resources of the greatest value" to blacks were regarded as:

	%
Skills training for job advancement	43
The franchise	19
A better education	16
Strong black leadership	10
Strong trade union	9
Strong political organization	3

Only 3 percent saw the role of trade unions as "working for political rights"; the vast majority saw them as a means of improving wages and working conditions.

Free Enterprise Versus Socialism

Schlemmer's respondents were asked who should own factories and shops in a black-ruled country: (1) the government; (2) black businessmen; or (3) anyone who can be successful in business, not only black people. The third option was chosen by 60 percent.

Proportions in the subsamples indicated that trade union members, "radical" workers with high-school education, and workers with experience in multinational corporations were substantially more likely to favor private enterprise. Groups least likely to see benefits in it were those in areas or companies with severe racial discrimination, those who were least skilled, and, to a lesser extent, those who had recently left school.

Schlemmer found that when various factors were taken into account, there was "virtually no support among black workers" for total disinvestment.

Orkin's Findings (1985)

Mark Orkin of the Community Agency for Social Enquiry conducted a survey into black attitudes toward disinvestment. His findings apparently differ dramatically from Schlemmer's. However, if the results are interpreted according to the same criteria as Schlemmer's, they are very similar.

Orkin's survey had 800 respondents in ten major metropolitan areas. Unfortunately, some of the questions are so misleading that the answers are not an accurate indication of anything.

According to the published "overview" of the findings, "more than three-quarters of respondents favor socialism over capitalism." The question on which this conclusion is based (Question 9) asks:

"Suppose South Africa had the government of your choice. There are two main patterns how it should organize people's work, and the ownership of factories and businesses. Which view do you most support?"

— the capitalist pattern in which businesses are owned and run by private businessmen, for their own profit.   22%

— the socialist pattern, in which workers have a say in the running of businesses, and share in the ownership and profits.   77%

This question is phrased in such a way that the only surprise lies in how many respondents chose the "capitalist" option. The definition of "socialism" corresponds more to the West German capitalistic "social market" economy than any dictionary definition of socialism.

The disinvestment question is inordinately long (225 + words), which frustrates the prospect of reliable responses. Also, it links the three options offered with people and groups. For instance, Bishop Tutu is listed as favoring restricted investment and Buthelezi, Oppenheimer, the government, and other homeland leaders are lumped together to represent the pro-investment position. The ANC, PAC, UDF, AZAPO, and some trade unions are listed as wanting no investment because it "only help(s) to keep apartheid alive and exploit Blacks."

Despite the lack of objectivity in the phraseology of the questions, the results were strikingly similar to Schlemmer's if properly interpreted.

They were as follows:

	Orkin		Schlemmer
	%		%
Pro-investment	26	}75	75
Conditionally pro-investment	49		
Anti-investment	24		25
Don't know	1		—

Orkin adds the 49 percent who were conditionally against investment to the 24 percent who were definitely against and comes up with 73 percent against investment. However, the section that 49 percent of the respondents checked says that "foreign firms should not be allowed to invest here unless they actively pressure the government to end apartheid, and recognize the trade unions chosen by the workers." Since virtually all foreign firms do meet with these requirements, we have put the 49 percent with the 26 percent in favor of investment.

The overview of Orkin's survey observes that 80 percent of respondents favor "one central government." But the only alternative offered to "a unitary arrangement in which all *blacks* and whites together vote for their leaders" was "a federal arrangement in which *Africans* are partly governed by homeland leaders, but also have some representation in central government" (our emphasis). Nonracial devolution, the most common form of democracy, was not offered.

When Orkin asked, "Which leader or organization would you most like to represent you in solving problems or grievances?" the response was as follows:

Mandela and the ANC	31%
Buthelezi and Inkatha	8%
Bishop Tutu	16%
UDF	8%
"other anti-investment organizations	6%
P. W. Botha and government	5%
"other pro-investment groups"	3%
other	3%
none	13%
don't know	8%

Other Surveys

Further conflicting results come from other surveys, presumably conducted among different groups of people and also affected by the attitudes of the researchers and the analysis of the results. (The December 6, 1985 issue of *The Financial Mail* cited a survey in which 7.5 percent of blacks chose P. W. Botha as their preferred leader.)

The referendums that have been held among homeland blacks have indicated overwhelmingly moderate attitudes. For instance, the Ciskei referendum on independence was carried by a 90 percent-plus majority in a 90 percent-plus turnout. (Critics alleged that the results were rigged.) Most of the homelands have had high turnouts at the polls and landslide victories for the ruling party.

In 1983 the Louw Commission undertook black opinion surveys (not yet published) in Ciskei and the Border Region. Questions were aimed at avoiding confusion, and care was taken to minimize the "lie factor." For example, there was a multiple choice question regarding who should be allowed to do business in Ciskei. Respondents could answer yes or no to any of the alternatives: Nobody, Ciskeians, Transkeians, Other Blacks, Afrikaners, English, Indians, Coloureds, Everybody. "Nobody" was rejected by 99 percent, so they were all in favor of some private enterprise. "Everybody" was endorsed by 78.2 percent.

Many other answers reflected an overwhelming endorsement of the free market position on *specific* policy, even though the same people did not necessarily endorse *generalized* propositions regarding "free enterprise." For instance, although 22 percent said they favored socialism and 7 percent Marxism,

- 77% opposed wage control
- 71% supported private urban land ownership
- 85% supported private rural land ownership
- 97% supported the right to go into business
- 84% supported the right to form trade unions

A great deal of further evidence showed that specific questions get "moderate" answers, while general or ideological questions elicit a good number (though not a majority) of radical answers.

Schlemmer's and Orkin's studies, which were conducted among urban blacks, reveal a minority of radicalized blacks. Rural and small town blacks are generally considered to be "traditional" in their attitudes in that they have strong tribal loyalty.

Many observers nonetheless believe that Mandela has become such a folk hero, and the ANC so much a symbol of "the black liberation struggle," that they would win an overwhelming majority in at least a first election. It may well be true that they would receive more support than opinion polls indicate. However, 28 percent of the national population is nonblack, which means (assuming that not many nonblacks would vote for them) that the ANC would need to win 70 percent of the black vote in order to gain 50 percent of the national vote, which seems highly unlikely by any analysis. It should also be remembered that most blacks, especially rural blacks, have a strong ethnic consciousness. Neither Zulus, Sothos, Xhosas, nor any of the other main black groups are likely to vote in substantial numbers for a leader from a group other than their own. This is not a fashionable view, but it is nonetheless true.

Add to this the fact that 4 million to 6 million blacks are followers of the Zion Christian Church, which has a moderate policy and leader, and we are led to the conclusion that most blacks would support moderate leaders, and that no single group has a chance of a clear majority.

Without referendums there is the risk and likelihood that politicians will act contrary to their voters' wishes. However, given referendums, all the evidence indicates that the vast majority of blacks will support freehold title, free trade, and free competition. The system we recommend does not depend on the outcome of one election, but on many elections and referendums on many policies, candidates, parties, and presidents.

All things considered, it seems clear that most South African blacks prefer free market economic policies and peaceful reform. A large number of blacks in the "radicalized" urban areas support fairly radical leaders and organizations, but espouse moderate policies.

White Attitudes

The results of white opinion polls indicate that most whites accept that "power-sharing with blacks is inevitable."

	All whites %	Afrikaners %	English-speakers %
Agree	67.3	59.1	81.6
Disagree	17.8	20.4	13.4
No Opinion	14.9	20.5	5.0

(Source: *Rapport*, November 1985)

APPENDIX III

Protection of Minorities in the Swiss System

SWITZERLAND'S NEWEST CANTON, JURA, is a particularly good example of how minority domination can be avoided in a canton system.

For nine centuries Jura was an autonomous unit of the Holy Roman Empire, but in the course of the nineteenth century it was split between France and the Swiss canton of Bern.

The official language of Swiss cantons and communities is traditionally the language spoken by the majority of the population. Occasionally there are two official languages, but this was not the case in German-dominated Bern. For various reasons an increasingly strong French-Juran separatist movement emerged.

The Bern government always protested that it spent more on each Juran (Jurans constituted 7 percent of the Bern population) than on any other citizen, and that they were better off than the average French-Swiss citizen. However, "what was really at stake was the identity and self-respect of the Jura."

The separatists did not want handouts, they wanted "the power to transform their economy so that it needed no subsidy." So they wanted a liberal constitution and liberal economic and social policies. The Bern government considered the idea "unthinkable," but by Swiss law the matter could be decided by the Jurans themselves.

Among the Jurans there was also a unionist movement that wanted to stay with Bern. To the ultra-democratic Swiss, this meant there should not be a simple majority referendum, but several referendums: one for Jura as a whole, one for each border community, and one for each district in which 20 percent of the electorate petitioned for it. Thus even within Jura there could be no majority domination. If the separatists were a minority in Jura as a whole, they could still get a new canton in those parts of Jura where they were the majority.

To gain support for union, the Bern government held its own referendum in which an overwhelming majority voted in favor of granting Jura "self-determination," but not independence. However, in 1974, the separatists gained a small majority (54.2 percent) in one of the highest turnouts in Swiss history (91.8 percent), thus achieving their goal.

In 1975, three French border districts voted to opt out of Jura, but in subsequent community referendums, eight border communities voted for the new canton and one for Bern.

Jura was to become independent. But this did not mean it would automatically become a member of the Swiss confederation. In 1978 there was a national referendum in which the majority of Swiss citizens voted to admit Jura as an additional Swiss canton.

NOTES

Terminology

In a country marked by racial dissension, words describing racial groups and government institutions quickly develop different connotations for different people. Consequently, it is almost impossible to avoid offending someone no matter what terminology is used. We have used the words that are most commonly used in South Africa, that we judged least likely to cause confusion, and that we believe are acceptable to most people.

1. BLACK SOUTH AFRICANS: THEIR RISE AND FALL

In this chapter we have drawn a great deal of information from Colin Bundy's book, *The Rise & Fall of the South African Peasantry*. This meticulously researched work provides a fascinating account of nineteenth century black farming. We recommend it highly.

1. Wilson, Monica and Leonard Thompson, eds., *A History of South Africa to 1870* (Cape Town: David Philip, 1982), p. 123.
2. Bundy, Colin, *The Rise & Fall of the South African Peasantry* (London: Heinemann, 1979), p. 33.
3. Bundy, p. 52. There is no precise way of calculating the present-day equivalent of currencies at various times in history. During the nineteenth century the value of the pound did not fluctuate a great deal. A conservative rule-of-thumb estimate is that £1 in the nineteenth century is equal to approximately R20 ($10) in 1986. We have provided

rough estimates of present-day equivalents for the convenience of lay readers.

4. Bundy, p. 54.
5. Bundy, p. 71.
6. Houghton, D. Hobart and Jenifer Dagut, *Source Material on the South African Economy*, vol. 1, 1860–1870 (Cape Town: Oxford University Press), pp. 201-219.
7. Bundy, p. 75.
8. Bundy, p. 77.
9. Bundy, p. 161.
10. Bundy, p. 141.
11. Bundy, p. 114.
12. Bundy, p. 136.
13. Bundy, p. 139.
14. Bundy, p. 116.
15. Bundy, p. 174.
16. Bundy, p. 192.

2.　THE RISE OF AFRIKANERDOM

1. Wilson and Thompson, p. 187.
2. Wilson and Thompson, p. 195.
3. Muller, C.F.J., *500 Years: A History of South Africa* (Cape Town: Academica, 1981), p. 99.
4. Walker, Eric, *A History of Southern Africa* (London: Longmans, Green, 1959), p. 199.
5. Muller, p. 158.
6. De Klerk, W.A., *The Puritans in Africa* (Middlesex: Pelican, 1976), p. 23.
7. Wilson and Thompson, p. 365.

3.　THE RISE OF APARTHEID

1. Böeseken, A.J., *Slaves and Free Blacks at the Cape 1658–1700* (Cape Town: Tafelberg, 1977), pp. 45,46.
2. Muller, p. 361.
3. Muller, p. 361.
4. O'Brien, Terence H., *Milner* (London: Constable, 1979).
5. Hutt, W.H., *The Economics of the Colour Bar* (London: Andre Deutsch, 1964), pp. 62,63.
6. Muller, p. 415.
7. Houghton and Dagut, p. 84.
8. Hutt, p. 80.

7. THE REDISTRIBUTION OF WEALTH

1. McGrath, M.D., *Racial Income Distribution in South Africa* (Natal University, 1977), and Nattrass, Jill, *Narrowing Wage Differentials and Income Distribution in South Africa,* 1977.
2. Adams, K.A.H., *Political Engineering* (Transactions of the South Africa Institute of Electrical Engineers, June 1979).
3. Tullock, Gordon, *Economics of Income Redistribution* (Boston: Kluwer-Nijhoff Publishing, 1983), p. 94.

8. AFFIRMATIVE ACTION

1. *The Fairmont Papers,* Black Alternatives Conference, Dec. 1980.

15. SOCIOECONOMIC SOLUTIONS

1. Evidence given to Native Affairs Commission, 1865.

BIBLIOGRAPHY

Adams, K.A.H., *Political Engineering* (Transactions of the S. A. Institute of Electrical Engineers, June 1979).

Ashworth, Georgina, ed., *World Minorities in the Eighties* (Middlesex: Quartermaine House, 1980).

100 Baiese dokumente by die studie van die Suid-Afrikaanse geskiedenis 1648–1961 (Johannesburg: Nasou Beperk, 1980).

Bauer, P.T., *Equality, the Third World and Economic Delusion* (London: Weidenfeld and Nicolson, 1981).

Becker, Gary S., *The Economics of Discrimination* (Chicago and London: University of Chicago Press, 1971).

Beckett, Denis, *Permanent Peace* (Johannesburg: Saga Press, 1985).

Berman, Harold J., *Justice in the USSR* (Cambridge, Massachusetts: Harvard University Press, 1963).

Boeseken, A.J., *Slaves and Free Blacks at the Cape 1658–1700* (Cape Town: Tafelberg, 1977).

Bundy, Colin, *The Rise & Fall of the South African Peasantry* (London: Heinemann, 1979).

Bulletin of Statistics, June 1975 (Pretoria: Department of Statistics).

Buthelezi, Mangosuthu Gatsha, *Power is Ours* (New York: Books in Focus, 1979).

Cranston, M., *What are Human Rights?* (London: Bodley, 1973).

Davenport, T.R.H., *South Africa: A Modern History* (Johannesburg: Macmillan S. A., 1978).

Davenport, T.R.H. and K.S. Hunt, *The Right to the Land* (Cape Town: David Phillip, 1974).

De Klerk, W.A., *The Puritans in Africa* (Middlesex: Pelican, 1976).

Depoliticising South Africa, papers and proceedings of 1984 Free Market Foundation Congress, Pretoria.

Elphick, Richard and Hermann Giliomee, eds., *The Shaping of South African Society, 1652–1820* (Cape Town: Longman, 1979).

Faith, Nicholas, *Safety in Numbers* (London: Hamish Hamilton, 1984).

The Fairmont Papers, Black Alternatives Conference, December 1980 (San Francisco: Institute for Contemporary Studies, 1981).

Friedman, David, *The Machinery of Freedom* (New York: Arlington House, 1978).

The Hammond Almanac, 1980 (Maplewood: Hammond Almanac Inc.).

Hayek, Friedrich A., *The Constitution of Liberty* (Chicago: Henry Regnery, 1972).

—————————, *Law, Legislation and Liberty*, (Chicago: University of Chicago Press, 1973).

Heldman, D.C., J.T. Bennett, and M.H. Johnson, *Deregulating Labour Relations* (Dallas: Fisher, 1981).

Hollyer, Beatrice, "Targets of Contrast," *Frontline:* vol. 5, no. 5 (April 1985).

Houghton, D. Hobart and Jenifer Dagut, *Source Material on the South African Economy*, vols. I–III (Cape Town: Oxford University Press, 1972/3).

Hutt, W.H., *The Economics of the Colour Bar* (London: Andre Deutsch, 1964).

Indicator South Africa, vol. 3, no. 1 (Winter, 1985) Centre for Applied Social Sciences, University of Natal.

Innes, Duncan, "The Real World of the Left" *Frontline:* vol. 5, no. 8 (August 1985).

Kantor, B. and D. Rees, *South African Economic Issues* (Johannesburg: Juta, 1982).

Malherbe, E. G., *Education in South Africa, 1652–1922* (Cape Town: Juta, 1925).

Markman, T., *Transport Policy* (Johannesburg: Free Market Foundation, 1984).

McGrath, M. D., *Racial Income Distribution in South Africa*, Interim Research Report No. 2 (Dept. of Economics, Natal University, 1977).

Mises, Ludwig von, *Human Action: A Treatise on Economics* (Chicago: Contemporary Books Inc., 3rd Revised Edition, 1966).

Planning for Freedom, (Illinois: Libertarian Press, 1980).

Muller, C. F. J., ed., *500 Years: A History of South Africa* (Cape Town: Academica, 1981).

Nattrass, Jill, "Narrowing Wage Differentials and Income Distribution in South Africa," *S. A. Journal of Economics*, vol. 45 (4), 1977.

Noble, John, *The Cape and South Africa Official Handbook* (Cape Town: Juta, 1981).

Nozick, Robert, *Anarchy, State and Utopia* (New York: Basic Books, 1974).

O'Brien, Terence H., *Milner* (London: Constable, 1979).

Occupational Licensing and the Supply of Non-Professional Labour, Manpower Monograph No. 11 (Washington, D.C.: Department of Labor, 1969).

Orkin, Mark, *Black Atitudes to Disinvestment: The Real Story* (Opinion Survey in conjunction with the Institute for Black Research).

Rabushka, Alvin, *A Theory of Racial Harmony* (South Carolina: University of South Carolina Press, 1974).

Race Relations Survey, vol. 38, 1984 (Johannesburg: S. A. Institute of Race Relations, 1985).

Rothbard, Murray, *Conceived in Liberty*, Vols I–IV (New Rochelle: Arlington House, 1975).

The Ethics of Liberty (Atlantic Highlands: Humanities Press, 1982).

Man, Economy & State (Los Angeles: Nash Publishing, 1970).

S. A. Reserve Bank Quarterly Bulletin, Sept. 1975.

Schlemmer, Lawrence, *Black Worker Attitudes* (Indicator Project, Centre for Applied Social Sciences, Durban, 1984).

Smith, Edward Conrad, *The Constitution of the United States* (New York: Barnes & Noble, 1979).

The South African Society: Realities and Future Prospects (Pretoria: HSRC, 1985).

Sowell, Thomas, *Race and Economics* (New York: David McKay, 1975).

Swart, N.J., *Chairman Report of the Commission of Inquiry into the Economic Development of the Republic of Ciskei* (Ciskei: Office of the Presidency, 1983).

Templeton, Kenneth S., ed., *The Politicization of Society* (Indianapolis: Liberty Press, 1979).

Thomas, Wolfgang H., *Labour Perspectives on South Africa* (Cape Town: David Philip, 1974).

Trade Union Directory, 1983–84 (Johannesburg: TUCSA).

Tullock, Gordon, *Economics of Income Redistribution* (Boston: Kluwer-Nijhoff Publishing, 1983).

Walker, Eric, *A History of Southern Africa*, 3rd edition (London: Longmans, Green, 1959).

Whittington, G.W. and J.B. McI. Daniel, *Problems of Land Tenure and Ownership in Swaziland.* Reprinted from *Environment and Land Use in Africa* (London: Methuen & Co. Ltd.).

Wilson, Monica and Leonard Thompson, eds., *A History of South Africa to 1870* (Cape Town: David Philip, 1982).

Williams, Walter E., *The State Against Blacks* (New York: McGraw-Hill, 1982).

_____, *America: A Minority Viewpoint* (Stanford: Hoover Institution Press, 1982).

INDEX